give methods a chance

the society pages

the
society
pages

give methods a chance

kyle green

UTICA COLLEGE

sarah lageson

RUTGERS UNIVERSITY-NEWARK

w. w. norton & company

NEW YORK | LONDON

W. W. Norton & Company has been independent since its founding in 1923, when William Warder Norton and Mary D. Herter Norton first published lectures delivered at the People's Institute, the adult education division of New York City's Cooper Union. The firm soon expanded its program beyond the Institute, publishing books by celebrated academics from America and abroad. By mid-century, the two major pillars of Norton's publishing program—trade books and college texts—were firmly established. In the 1950s, the Norton family transferred control of the company to its employees, and today—with a staff of four hundred and a comparable number of trade, college, and professional titles published each year—W. W. Norton & Company stands as the largest and oldest publishing house owned wholly by its employees.

Book Design: Isaac Tobin
Composition: Westchester Book Composition
Manufacturing: LSC Crawfordsville
Production Manager: Sean Mintus

ISBN: 978-1-324-00054-9

W. W. Norton & Company, Inc., 500 5th Avenue, New York, NY 10110
wwnorton.com

W. W. Norton & Company Ltd., 15 Carlisle Street, London W1D 3B5

3 4 5 6 7 8 9 0

thesocietypages.org

contents

series preface

DOUGLAS HARTMANN AND CHRISTOPHER UGGEN

t started with a conversation about record labels. Our favorite imprints are known for impeccable taste, creative design, and an eye for both quality and originality. Wouldn't it be cool if W. W. Norton & Co. and TheSocietyPages.org joined forces to develop a book series with the same goals in mind? Namely, to consistently deliver the best work by the most original voices in the field.

The Society Pages (TSP) is a multidisciplinary, online hub bringing fresh social scientific knowledge and insight to the broadest public audiences in the most open, accessible, and timely manner possible. The largest, most visible collection of sociological material on the Web, TSP is composed of a family of prolific blogs and bloggers, podcasts, interviews, exchanges, teaching content, reading recommendations, and original features like There's Research on That (TROT!), Office Hours,

Clippings, and Discoveries. The TSP book series, published in collaboration with W. W. Norton, assembles the best original content from the Web site in key thematic collections. With contributions from leading scholars and a provocative collection of discussion topics and group activities, this innovative series provides an accessible and affordable entry point for strong sociological perspectives on topics of immediate social import and public relevance.

Volume 7 of the book series shows us how sociologists actually do the work we feature on TSP. *Give Methods a Chance* is based on the popular podcast series of the same name, founded and hosted by Kyle Green of Utica College and Sarah Lageson of Rutgers University–Newark. Before pouring their formidable energies into the Give Methods a Chance podcast in 2015 (also hosted on TSP), Green and Lageson were key figures in building and shaping both TSP and its Office Hours podcast. Their book thus offers a unique multimedia introduction to research methods, in which key material is organized on the page and full-length podcasts are online for further exploration at TheSocietyPages.org /methods.

In this volume, Green and Lageson introduce readers to 19 podcasts with some of the most creative, exciting, and influential researchers in sociology. Some are already famous, others up-and-coming, and each brings a distinctive approach and powerful tools for studying the social world. Readers will gain new insight into studies like Devah Pager's famous social experiments on discrimination, C. J. Pascoe's ethnographic immersion in a working-class high school, and Deborah Carr's longitudinal surveys that continue tracking such teenagers for the full duration of their lives. They will learn how researchers like Vincent Roscigno and Matthew Hughey mix and match methods to address sets of interrelated questions. And they will also understand how (and why) sociologists such as Daniel Sui, Naomi Sugie, and Francesca Polletta are gaining insights from big data, smartphone surveys, and online forums, respectively.

Together, these pieces reveal both the big-picture issues in research and the little details that can make or break a study. The text and complementary podcasts offer a distinctive, first-person window into how sociologists generate knowledge: the fun, the headaches, the workarounds, and the care and passion needed to get things right.

Green and Lageson first approached us about doing this volume after encountering a textbook they described as "great as far as methods books go," by which they meant it was "long, dry, overly detailed, and expensive." Perhaps their greatest frustration was that most methods texts lacked readable and exciting examples of the methodologies that we are trying to teach. So they created a podcast series and wrote this book to help convey the excitement and innovation in producing sociological knowledge, as well as the tough choices researchers make in the field.

This overriding mission of *Give Methods a Chance* is wholly congruent with our TSP mission of making sociology accessible to broader audiences. Until now, however, we have rarely given research methods a front-stage role on the site or in our books. This is because so much writing on methodology is prepared by and for experts, rather than students, journalists, policy makers, or the general public. But research methods have always played a prominent role in our backstage editorial discussions about what to highlight on our site and in our volumes. This is because every study featured as a Discovery or called out in our white papers or There's Research on That! must be built on a solid base of evidence. In particular, we take pains to be certain that the type of claim sociologists are making about the world is well matched to the data that they collect and the methods they use to analyze it.

Give Methods a Chance is organized into four sections: Interpretive and Qualitative Methods, Explanatory and Quantitative Methods, Mixed Methods, and Innovations. This straightforward organizational scheme will map seamlessly onto existing texts and syllabi in research methodology, introductory sociology, and capstone courses, while the content uniquely conveys the voices of researchers. What is equally apparent in these pages is the editorial vision of Green and Lageson—outstanding teachers and researchers as well as gifted interviewers who help render all this sociological expertise accessible without getting bogged down in jargon or technique.

Before we turn things over to Professors Green and Lageson, we want to express our gratitude, as always, to the University of Minnesota, W. W. Norton & Co. (in particular, the sociology editor, Sasha Levitt, and her predecessor, Karl Bakeman), and our associate editor and producer Letta Page. The Society Pages's graduate student board (and current graduate editor, Jacqui Frost) plays an important part in everything we do at TSP. But this project is special, as Green and Lageson are two former board members who have taken their passion for public scholarship to the next level. Their *Give Methods a Chance* book and podcast series wonderfully represent TSP, while giving voice to their distinctive vision of sociological research and teaching.

introduction: how the sociological sausage is made

KYLE GREEN AND SARAH LAGESON

Many an academic has struggled to "reach the masses" beyond the "ivory tower." Conferences are convened, plenary speeches are given, and academic journals are organized around the theme of "public" sociology. Yet, it's a difficult and challenging task to bring research away from the academy, and even when a study *does* make this important journey, the way its findings were found—originating ideas, failures, and methodological considerations—are left behind.

Sometimes, this is the result of a journalist pushing a particular finding for reader appeal, and other times it's because people simply believe research methods are too technical, dry, or boring for the public. The methods behind knowledge creation remain the "black box" of the social sciences, full of information but hidden from sight behind steep paywalls and dense, technical academic writing.

Even undergraduates ostensibly interested in social sciences tend to dread the required semester or two of research methods. But, can we blame them? Some textbooks can be overly simplistic, while some can leave readers lost in a maze of details. "Methods" becomes a collection of memorized terms and rules rather than a challenging, exciting, and fulfilling practice of discovery. This effectively channels students toward caring more about their topical courses than the fundamental skills that unite the divergent group of scholars who make up the social sciences. Overlooking the messy, interesting details of what research really looks like in the field means textbooks often fail to communicate how top-tier research is done.

Whether intentional or unintentional, it is a significant loss that obscures the process of research. Learning about methodologies and how knowledge is constructed is irreplaceable for developing critical thinking—the often-celebrated, but ever-elusive quality that liberal arts programs strive to instill in students. At its best, an understanding of research methods can provide the tools and desire to engage with and understand the macro-level forces that shape our society, as well as the micro-level, everyday experiences of ourselves and others.

In a matter of minutes, anyone can access countless blogs, newspaper articles, and online encyclopedias, and, from the paranormal to the reactionary, evidence can be garnered for virtually any stance. This can be a liberating, overwhelming, and debilitating experience. An understanding of good research can help turn down the firehose of often-contradictory or flat-out wrong ideas by providing the skills and skepticism necessary to evaluate the strength of the argument, the source of the data, and the analytical techniques behind the conclusions.

Perhaps most importantly, an understanding of methods means acknowledging what you do not know—and knowing which questions will help you find an answer.

this book

This book is a collection of short, accessible pieces that describe a variety of research methods through the experiences and recollections of prominent sociologists. These stories from the field are designed to demystify the research process and show how methods are put into action. Our conversations allow researchers to share useful tricks-of-the-trade, engage in honest discussions about the little details that led to things going right (or wrong), and provide first-hand accounts from a mix of established scholars and young, cutting-edge practitioners.

Our goal is not to "pretty up" or "dumb down" methods. Rather, we bring the reader backstage as scholars make key decisions and adapt to challenges, from struggling to access a key research site to realizing an important aspect of data is missing. We believe these stories from the field not only add interest, but a more thorough account of how seminal works of social science get done. It sets realistic expectations for young sociologists wondering what research actually looks like.

This volume builds on podcast interviews available on "Give Methods a Chance" at TheSocietyPages.org. The podcast format ensures a conversational tone, creating a text that is accessible and inviting to a diverse range of students. It also cuts down on jargon while focusing on the process of research. In addition, students and instructors can access the full interview recording—an option that has proven popular in the contemporary college environment (including in our own courses).

structure

Each section of this book—Interpretive and Qualitative, Explanatory and Quantitative, Mixed Methods, and Innovations—is prefaced by a short introduction that explains the methodological grouping and provides a short summary of each interview.

These sections are organized around both the researcher's epistemological goal—the way in which they construct knowledge—*and* the type of data generated. Various approaches to organization hold value, but we seek an approach that better reveals the messy back-and-forth between the topic of interest, the questions researchers ask, the methods they choose to answer those questions, and the data these methods create. In the majority of existing methods textbooks, the divisions between methodological approaches, research goals, and data types are clean and seemingly absolute: you either use numbers or you don't; you are either looking to describe a phenomenon or explain why it happens; you are either conducting an ethnography or you are administering surveys. In these texts, both the method and the data seem to exist in an ahistorical vacuum. This certainly makes things easier, especially in the classroom. However, in the field, things are rarely so clean. Decisions are pragmatic and frequent.

In this vein, the first section of our book engages scholars who employ an array of qualitative approaches to better understand the social world. In each example, researchers choose a methodological approach that generates qualitative data because they seek to interpret and make sense of the production and exchange of meaning and cultural values.

We share stories of researchers using interviews, focus groups, and ethnographic studies. We also follow researchers as they seek insight into how culture works by unpacking the meanings buried within archival documents and contemporary advertisements.

In the second section, we bring together scholars who use quantitative approaches to transform the social world into analyzable data sets. While some quantitative-based studies focus on the descriptive, these researchers privilege explanation *and* description by isolating variables, seeking to understand the relationships between them, and, in some cases, attempting to tease out cause and effect. Some seek to bring the experimental methods most commonly associated with the lab into the complex and difficult-to-control social world, while others construct large data sets for statistical analysis, or gather data on the same set of participants over time to explain life course patterns.

In the third section, we turn to scholars who use multiple methods within a single study, often drawing on both quantitative and qualitative data, and employing elements of the exploratory, descriptive, interpretive, and explanatory. Some of our contributors seek to confirm their findings by approaching the same question or cultural object from multiple methodological angles; others use different methods to get at different aspects of the social questions they seek to answer.

Finally, we look at new and exciting methodological innovations with a group of scholars pushing the field forward, using new technologies to gather previously inaccessible data, examining new virtual communities and online spaces of communication, and employing methods from outside the discipline in creative ways. Taken together, these studies capture the excitement of working on the cutting edge of sociology, while reminding us that even the most innovative approaches still face the most persistent methodological challenges.

We hope that as readers work their way through our collection, they come to realize that the arrangement of these sections is to a certain extent arbitrary. The book would have looked different if we organized the chapters strictly based on types of data. Another approach might have been to organize the book by the topic under study. For example, we can see a number of variations of visual and textual analysis across the sections. And, because researchers rarely stay within the lines when conducting actual research, many of the chapters could have easily fit in another section. This is not a cause for concern. Rather, it should remind the reader that the best researchers seek the best ways to answer the questions that excite them and let this pursuit guide them.

the simple pleasures

We began the Give Methods a Chance podcast with the humble goal of providing scholars a platform to discuss their research approach in a way that was not only useful to those interested in practicing or learning about methods, but also enjoyable to listen to. As our interviews grew in number and scope, we noticed two key commonalities: the joy scholars found in putting a research methodology into practice and their appreciation of what we might consider the more mundane aspects of research.

Expressing delight with the process of research in an academic journal might seem indulgent, superfluous, and, most damning, unscientific. Yet, repeatedly, when we gave researchers a chance to "sell" the method of their choosing, our guests spoke with enthusiasm and affection. Ethnographers discussed the thrill of entering a site for the first time, focus group moderators reflected on the privilege of guiding a group through a discussion of a complicated issue, and interviewers spoke of the emotional connections formed during research. The quantitatively inclined shared the excitement of recognizing an emergent theme in the coding or discovering significant findings in a regression model.

In some cases, the source of that joy was more obvious— hanging out with surfers on scenic, hidden Australian beaches or cracking a code to discover a previously unknown legal document. In others, it was a sort of delayed gratification, like answering big questions about social class only after combing through archival data showing where elite members of society sat when enjoying the orchestra. The best researchers find the method that is right for their biggest questions, making the long and often grueling process of study a source of wonder and elucidation.

Good research comes from researchers who take care, if not delight, in the technical process of study. The dramatic findings, the emotional confessions, and the unexpected statistical results sometimes represent the tiniest fractions of time spent doing research. Yet, in talking through their research experience, our podcast guests also demonstrate affection for the moments others might find most difficult. Their appreciation of the potentially confounding or tedious transcended any and all disciplinary divides. We hope these stories from the field succeed in capturing this excitement and inspiring others to find the method that brings them the same joy.

But really, all we can hope is that you, dear reader, will give methods a chance.

part 1: interpretive and qualitative methods

Researchers turn to *qualitative methods* to better understand the values and behaviors that make up our social worlds. A number of popular methodologies fall under the label "qualitative." These include (but are not limited to) interviews, focus groups, and ethnography. Each method involves the researcher making direct contact with the social phenomena under study, such as a cultural practice, ritual, or research participant. The researcher then systematically transforms these experiences into data. With qualitative work, concepts often emerge from the field rather than mapping onto predetermined variables.

Due to the flexibility of qualitative work, such methods are well suited for *exploratory* first steps. Here researchers are able to gain information about a new topic, see if a phenomenon of interest is possible to study, or begin to formulate questions. But this isn't always the case.

Qualitative work is also particularly suited to more in-depth *interpretive* approaches. *Interpretive* approaches position meaning-making practices at the center of inquiry. While qualitative research is not always interpretive and interpretive work is not always qualitative, the two often go hand in hand. In a sense, qualitative researchers operate in the space between the more "science" side of the discipline—the search for objective descriptions of institutions, social structures, and behaviors—and more journalistic or artistic forays into the subjective-life worlds of groups and peoples.

Interviews offer a way to gather basic facts and gain insight into behavior where observation may be difficult or even impossible. Through engaging in a series of questions and answers with study participants, researchers can learn about representations, identity, boundary work, cultural ideals, and emotional states as well as how people understand and experience the world around them. *Focus groups* are planned discussions designed to elicit a participant's opinion on a particular topic. Unlike interviews, a group of people are brought together to have a free-flowing conversation that ideally offers a glimpse into the way people talk together to construct meaning. *Ethnographic* research is based on observing and interacting with people in their natural settings. Researchers head out into the world, and approaches to ethnography range from full participation and immersion in a group, movement, or subculture to detached observation with no interaction.

Some qualitative researchers employ these methods to get an accurate view of the behaviors people engage in and the lives they live. Others are trying to learn about the *construction* of meaning and give their readers entry into the subjective experiences of the people and phenomena they are studying. In both cases, the qualitative researcher typically seeks a *depth* of knowledge not readily available through other methodologies. Talking with people, for instance, can reveal emotional dimensions that are impossible to access in other ways. Having groups of people discuss an issue gives us a glimpse into the process through which people work through ideas, draw on different forms of expertise, and place themselves within larger cultural narratives. Observation and participation allows understandings of the interactions, behaviors, and context that make up community but might remain invisible in data gleaned from other methodological approaches.

The qualitative approach will seem familiar to journalists who employ similar techniques or gather related forms of data and information. However, in the academic setting, the empirical questions and focus are guided by previous research and existing bodies of theory. The goal is rarely to simply understand or describe a phenomenon in itself.

Qualitative study also requires an emphasis on systematic data collection. Sometimes, this might look like researchers just asking questions, having a conversation, watching people, or even trying out a new activity; still, the process must be structured in a manner that allows other scholars to understand the context, make sense of the data, and possibly even reproduce the study at a later date to look for continuity and change.

The interactive nature of qualitative methodologies raises a number of issues before, during, and after the research process. *Positionality*, or how the researcher's own identity and background shape their perceptions of the field of study or how their presence might alter the field of study, is a key aspect of qualitative work. Researchers must appreciate the power dynamic that exists between observer and participant and recognize the emotional connections formed in the field. Researchers, then, lay along a spectrum from those who do their best to maintain *objectivity* as detached observers simply recording the facts to researchers who fully enter the field, embedding in and embracing the *subjective* experience as a path to understanding.

Interpretive, qualitative approaches can also be applied in textual and visual analysis. Here, scholars study culture through two of the fundamental mediums for the representation and sharing of ideas about the world. The underlying premise is that the way the world is rendered into text-based and visual-based representations is never innocent, and critical analysis will help us understand how culture works and how it is deployed.

In this section, we introduce five common qualitative approaches through discussions with venerable sociologists and up-and-coming scholars. Each provides an example of interpretive scholarship done well.

Amy Schalet introduces us to *in-depth interviews* through her comparative research on the understanding and management of adolescent sexuality in the United States and the Netherlands. Schalet shows that topic and the researcher's autobiography often determine the most suitable research method and study design, and our discussion helps illustrate how interviews reveal both shared and different cultural understandings. Schalet also addresses the obstacles a researcher navigates when exploring a sensitive topic (here, teen sexuality).

Audrey Kobayashi discusses *focus groups* in her work on the experiences and understandings of citizenship among Canadian immigrants from Hong Kong. Kobayashi's work employs a method common to the marketing and advertising worlds, but underutilized within the social sciences. In particular, talking with Kobayashi shows how focus groups can provide insight into the dynamic process through which communities forge a sense of identity together. Kobayashi also shares a number of practical tips for researchers that can make the difference between a successful and failed focus group.

C. J. Pascoe shares her approach to *ethnographic research* and her experience studying gender and sexuality in a diverse, working-class high school. Pascoe's immersion into a high school setting is particularly useful in considering positionality as she gets in trouble with hall monitors and attempts to convince the girls' basketball team that she is worthy of their respect.

Madison Van Oort and Kyle Green employ a semiology- and discourse-based form of *visual analysis* to study Super Bowl commercials. The researchers highlight the importance of creativity and developing a "good eye" for how symbols take on particular meaning and reveal ideological messages conveyed through advertising. This conversation helps us understand how being transparent about the researcher's background plays an important role in building the trust of the reader.

David FitzGerald and David Cook-Martín take us into the archives to discuss *comparative historical research*. In their project, FitzGerald and Cook-Martín analyze legal records from 22 countries to challenge the widely held view that, in the long run, democracy and racism cannot coexist. They code long-term trends in immigration law and employ qualitative analysis to better understand how and why they found the particular patterns they did.

interviews and telling a good story

FEATURING AMY SCHALET

nterviews offer a way to gather basic factual data and gain insight into behavior where observation may be difficult, or even impossible. While not achieving the immersion into the field that ethnographers seek, interviews provide valuable insight into representations, identity, boundary work, cultural ideals, and emotional states.

Interviews range from extremely structured—where interviewers stick exclusively to their question guide—to the unstructured—where interviewers engage in a conversation with respondents that is loosely guided by predetermined topics. In some ways, highly structured interviews begin to take on the format of survey research, albeit in a more flexible and personal way. In contrast, unstructured interviews might take on some ethnographic qualities, where the researcher is able to adapt to the field and the respondents. When structuring an interview, researchers must choose whether to emphasize depth versus breadth. While unstructured interviews provide depth, structured interviews tend to allow for more breadth, where researchers prioritize increasing the quantity of subjects rather than extending time with a single participant.

Amy Schalet's qualitative work masterfully illustrates the strengths of semistructured in-depth interviews to address a somewhat taboo topic: adolescent sexuality. In her approach, the interview method gradually introduces research participants into this topic through building rapport in a friendly, one-on-one setting. The data she collects are both bolstered by and communicated through storytelling. By asking good questions and writing accessible findings, Schalet digs into the background beliefs of participants and points readers toward how context, culture, and class shape our understanding of social issues.

To do this project, Schalet conducted over 130 interviews with secular or moderately Christian, white middle-class parents and teenagers in the United States and the Netherlands. She draws out key differences in the way the two respective cultures conceptualize teenage sexuality. They are starkly different. In the Netherlands, adolescent sexuality is viewed as part of the natural process of maturation that should be guided, but not admonished, by moral rules. In the United States, adolescent sexuality is viewed as both an uncomfortable topic of conversation and a problem to be prevented. Even more, Schalet reveals how these two different understandings of teenage sexuality are part and parcel of the two countries' distinct cultural understandings of individualism, personal freedom, and personal sacrifice.

talking about the taboo

Schalet defines in-depth interviewing as having a conversation with people that gets beyond just "what they do" and their superficial opinions. To access subjects' underlying assumptions and belief systems, she crafts her interviews to uncover the social processes her interviewees participate in, pushing them toward deeper levels of reflection. "On the one hand, it is informal," she says, "like a conversation you would have with a friend. But, it is different because you do a lot more listening than you would with a friend. [Yet], it is the same, because if you are being a good friend, you really lean in in order to hear what they are saying."

Schalet's work falls in between the extremely structured interview, where interviewers stick to their predetermined questions, and the unstructured interview, where interviewers conduct more of a loosely guided conversation. She allows for some of the flexibility and emotional resonance of the ethnographic approach while maintaining the consistency and breadth of interviews.

Although conducting interviews from two different countries allowed Schalet to draw comparisons between Dutch and American understandings of adolescent sexuality, it was essential that the two countries she chose for her research share enough commonalities to justify cross-national analysis. In this case, Schalet explains, the countries have a surprising amount in common: both are relatively wealthy Western countries with similar understandings of adolescent life and a similar cultural history steeped in Protestant values and changed by a sexual revolution in the 1960s and 1970s. Schalet is also particularly well positioned to conduct research on these two countries, having lived in both during her formative years. This "first-order" knowledge gives Schalet a level of familiarity that helps her understand and translate the culture of youth sexuality from the Dutch perspective. Yet, she's not so much of an insider that the ideas would seem boring and not worthy of examination.

As she constructed her method to reveal cross-cultural differences, Schalet had to ensure that her results were not the outcome of poor sampling or of comparing groups that were differently positioned within their respective countries. To ensure that she was not "comparing apples to oranges," Schalet sought to make each sample as similar as possible: "The samples can't be 'representative,' because it is not a random sample. But they have to be typical of the country. . . . I went for the moderate middle. I looked only at the middle class, only at white people, and only at not very religious people. I went for locations that weren't extremes."

recruiting interview subjects

Studying a sensitive topic can make recruitment difficult. For this reason, Schalet made sure to emphasize that the study was about a lot more than just sex. "Instead, I said it was about what it is like to grow up, dealing with lots of different topics. So I deflected the potential controversy." In this case, Dutch schools were happy to open their doors, while many U.S. schools worried about courting scandal. Schalet had to rely on personal connections and a bit of luck when it came to the latter. "I got access to one of the most important schools through total accident. Someone on the school board saw the word Dutch [in the project description] and had Dutch heritage."

Beyond recruiting, the sensitive nature of the topic also presented particular challenges. For instance, "within the United States, teen sexuality is so much more stigmatized for girls. Doing in-depth interviews is hard because, for them, even being asked about their sexuality seems like you are suggesting that they are sexual, which means they may be bad."

This sensitive topic required the researcher to be aware of the potential for emotional responses. Experienced qualitative researchers know how essential it is to build rapport with interview subjects so that they can discuss personal topics. Schalet, for her part, recommends beginning with the easy-to-answer questions before getting more personal. A researcher also needs to know when it's time to skip a question or return to a less-charged topic. Schalet said, for instance, that she would purposely *not* ask parents about the prospect of their own teenage child getting pregnant if the parent had earlier said anything like, "if she came home pregnant, she would no longer be my daughter." Schalet knew from experience she already had the data she needed in that situation.

"In-depth interviewing does require taking people to the edge of comfort. But, you also have to not just drop a bomb on them. If they said something like, 'he would be dead meat' or 'he shouldn't even come home,' then I would have to say something like, 'is there a circumstance where you could imagine that?' Then, 'maybe if they were engaged?' You have to take them back to their comfort zone. . . . You have to make them feel like even though they just had an explosion emotionally, you are with them."

reporting and applying interview findings

Not surprisingly, sexuality is a topic that attracts an audience beyond academia. Schalet's research has appeared in or been covered by *The New York Times*, *Washington Post*,

CNN, *Atlantic Monthly*, the BBC, and *Time*. She suspects that the attention goes beyond the prurient, though: qualitative interviews mean a researcher has the data to build and tell a compelling and relatable sociological story. Further, her findings present an intriguing alternative to the dominant cultural narrative about young Americans and unintended pregnancy. In her words, "I ultimately wanted my research to be available to people raising young people, as well as people dealing with issues of sexuality and youth in the political realm. . . . When I started doing this research, whenever people would talk about teen sexuality, they would often think of 'welfare queens' and out-of-wedlock birth. An implicit assumption was that you are talking about minorities, and that they are the only ones having teen sex. I wanted to pull away from this and look at the dominant population of the white middle class."

Both academic and nonacademic audiences can find something gripping in following the path of a single individual from beginning to end or in hearing a detailed account of an important human experience. The sociological story can also achieve emotional resonance where abstract analysis might fail. For Schalet, who explicitly wanted to speak beyond academia, "in-depth interviewing allows you to speak to broader audiences because it gives you great stories to tell. I start every chapter in the book with a story. That is a way to get journalists to read it and to hold on to the interest of a broader public."

In contrast to journalists, a social scientist uses stories to make broader connections. Schalet calls qualitative work "sociology that helps you interpret the story and connect it to the larger structures." There are, of course, limitations to the method. An in-depth interviewer cannot tell every story or consider all people. For Schalet, this meant a careful balance between going in-depth with her controlled but limited sample, or extending outward. "I have to make these choices about who I am going to focus on. There are whole groups whose stories you are not telling. I can't tell you much about the black middle class or the American working class. So there is a limit to whose story you tell! You can tell a good story, but not everyone's."

At its best, the in-depth interview deftly weaves together the micro and macro, the subjective and objective. The product is an engrossing work that shows how specific people channel and make sense of specific cultural values and norms, as seen in Schalet's use of primary data from interviews to make connections between the culture and control in the "private realm" of the family and the "public realm" of policy and the welfare state.

getting focus groups right

FEATURING AUDREY KOBAYASHI

ocus groups provide a semistructured setting for people to respond to questions, share their views, and engage in discussion. The method bears much in common with interviews; however, rather than examining one person's experiences and feelings, the researcher facilitates conversation among a group of participants. In this way, researchers pursue one of the fundamental contributions of sociology: to reveal how interpersonal and other relationships shape identities and worldviews.

In a focus group, researchers can see how people work through and construct ideas as a collective, whether or not they reach consensus. The data come not only from what people say about a topic, but how they work together to say it. Participants can also take more control of the conversation—asking questions of each other, stimulating new ideas, and even changing others' views.

Focus groups are widely used outside of academia to better understand public opinion, strategize political campaigns, test marketing campaigns, and even try out music for dogs. Our discussion with Audrey Kobayashi reveals why more researchers should consider making use of this dynamic methodological approach and provides us with a number of valuable "tricks of the trade" to ensure successful focus groups.

the study

Kobayashi's research is on the experience of recent Canadian immigrants from Hong Kong and their changing understanding of citizenship during the transition. In particular, Kobayashi and her research team are trying to better understand the transnational experiences of the several hundred-thousand people who migrated to Vancouver and Toronto from 1989 to 1997.

As seen throughout this book, good research means a close alignment between the topic, the types of questions being asked, and the chosen methodology. As Kobayashi explains with regard to her work, "because 'citizenship' is such a dynamic concept, it's not very effective to simply interview people one-on-one and say: 'How do you understand citizenship?' We would rather get that discursive sense of how people discuss citizenship and understand it among themselves."

Similarly, Kobayashi believes, as do many sociologists, that identity is contested and shaped by contextual factors, especially in communities with a common bond or shared culture. With focus groups, the researcher can see this identity work in action: "We hear first-hand from people about the experiences, but also, how other people react. People will compare their experiences, they'll sometimes challenge one another, or they will sometimes corroborate those experiences so that we have a sense not only of what the experiences are, but how they're actually lived and negotiated." She continues, "Overall, it means that the focus group allows us to uncover the actual discourses through which common identity is developed, and through which it is negotiated, challenged, and maintained."

Due to the dynamic qualities of focus groups, Kobayashi was able to observe often-elusive community sentiments. For instance, previous research had not revealed the resentment that Canadian-born Chinese college students had toward those born in Hong Kong or the processes through which they attempted to differentiate the two groups by establishing themselves as first and foremost Canadian. She complicated the idea of assimilation by revealing how community definitions of citizenship and belonging are constantly renegotiated, rejected, and embraced.

tips and tricks

A focus group seems like a rather straightforward undertaking: ask a few questions, let the group talk. But the method offers a particular challenge to the researcher. Instead of an ethnographer building one-on-one rapport or immersing themselves in an unfamiliar life world, the focus group moderator facilitates and encourages interaction through a careful balance of a loose format and scientific restraint. Like a good instructor in the classroom, the facilitator ensures everyone has the space to speak, while not forcing people to voice their opinion. The goal is to keep the conversation a *conversation*, rather than a "group interview" with respondents each taking a turn answering the same question.

In Kobayashi's experience, a good focus group requires a facilitator to lead the discussion and a research assistant to document the interactions and ensure recording and audio equipment is functioning properly and with as little disruption as possible. The participants must, Kobayashi says, know that they have the full attention and the engagement of the facilitator, and that can't happen if she is typing, taking notes, or checking the sound equipment.

Who gets invited to the table is, of course, crucial as well. Kobayashi made sure that each group was organized strategically and according to some shared background or commonality. For example, she interviewed students (and youth in general) separately from older generations. In other cases, depending on the topic, groups might be separated by gender.

Of course, because of the fluid nature of the question and answer, there is always the danger that one or two group members will dominate the conversation. If this happens, the facilitator should have a strategy in place to pull the conversation back and allow others to share. Kobayashi always has a few questions ready for quiet participants: "a warm-up question; nothing too personal, something like 'When did you come to Canada?' Of course, we know that from the questionnaire, but it allows people to just get into the conversation and start talking about it." While these prompt questions might not provoke the dynamic exchanges needed for data collection, it is a useful strategy to change the direction of the conversation or get the whole focus group involved.

There is, you may have noticed, a great deal of value in attending to the mundane elements of focus group preparation. These rarely discussed preparations allow a dynamic, free-flowing conversation that touches on often-difficult subjects. Again, much like in teaching, the room matters: "You need to have a comfortable setting where people are going to feel that they belong and that they can speak freely. We usually use the offices of community associations, but sometimes a restaurant or another organization."

Further, since multiple people will arrive at the same time, researchers must convey professionalism by having set out questionnaires and other materials for group participants and having their equipment set up and tested. This also removes last-minute pressures that might preoccupy the moderator. Kobayashi insists, too, that each seat have a name card so that participants can refer to one another by name. These small details remove impediments and set up focus groups for success.

Even putting out snacks falls under the purview of the moderator! Kobayashi explains, "People are going to need drinks, and we usually try to provide some food as well, but the food needs to be something that's not going to provide a lot of crunchiness, that isn't in cellophane wrapping (these are very minor things, but they can really mess up your recordings), as well as putting drinks in soft containers like paper cups so that they're not banging on the table."

Each practical detail comes together for quality results. The more small things that go wrong, the more likely the conversation will devolve into a group interview—a method that Kobayashi describes as simply being "a mish-mash of bits and pieces of information that is very difficult to set up analytically." Done right, however, the focus group offers unparalleled access to the process of conversation and the social construction of meaning.

negotiating the
ethnographic hallways

FEATURING C. J. PASCOE

E thnography involves a researcher entering a social scene or culture to better understand it. This embedded position gives a unique look into the process of meaning construction, group division and connection, and the messiness of building identities. In other words, the ethnographer writes about how and what people do rather than how and what they *say* they do.

Ethnographic approaches range from observing a group by remaining on the outside and seeking to hold onto a level of objectivity, to full immersion, with a researcher even using his or her own body as a tool to better understand the actual experiences of the group under study. Contemporary ethnographers are pushed to reflexively consider their position in the field, how it may have shaped the way others acted in relation to the researcher, and their interpretation of those actions.

On the spectrum of methodological options, all forms of ethnography (whether more participant or more observer) involve the highest level of sustained contact between the researcher and the field. Because "getting your hands dirty" is a prerequisite of good ethnography, access and the relationship between the researcher and the participants are powerful currency.

C. J. Pascoe's research for her book *Dude, You're a Fag: Masculinity and Sexuality in High School* demonstrates how ethnography can help us better understand cultural shifts in masculinity and provide insight into how people—in this case high school boys—can present many types of seemingly contradictory identities. For instance, the boys of Pascoe's research describe themselves as being supportive of gay people while *also* casually using homophobic insults (like the word "fag" to signal inadequate masculinity rather than homosexuality). Here, Pascoe uses her research to discuss the challenges of finding and accessing a research site, the importance of being aware of your positionality, and the joys of ethnography.

the project

When Pascoe first began her fieldwork, she wanted to know how today's teenage boys understood and enacted masculinity. While previous research in this vein considered multiple waves of feminist activism and changing cultural norms of femininity, Pascoe noticed that scholars' understanding of cultural changes around masculinity were relatively paltry. Plus, Pascoe's previous attempts to understand the topic through interview methods had left her dissatisfied.

The problem was not that young men refused to talk (though many predicted that would happen). In fact, they were happy to talk, Pascoe recalls. "They told me all sorts of interesting stories, they were very vulnerable in our conversations. However, it was almost as if they were answering in ways they expected a Berkeley researcher to approve of." For instance, Pascoe would observe young men homophobically harass one another, but when she engaged them in an interview, they would perform a different style of masculinity: "this sort of new-age sensitive guy, kinder, gentler masculinity." Ethnography offered Pascoe a way to see how young men performed and lived out their masculinity, rather than how they explained it.

finding the site

Once you have a topic and a method, the next challenge is finding a site for fieldwork. For Pascoe, a researcher of childhood and youth culture, this is particularly tough. "We live in an incredibly age-graded society where kids and adults are really kept separate from one another. Kids are really sort of kept confined to private spaces. We really keep them out of public spaces, presumably for their own safety, but also I think as a form of control."

Pascoe did not particularly want to conduct her ethnography in a school, but there weren't a lot of other options. "Well, I could go to a video game parlor; those still sort of existed when I was doing this research at the beginning. I could go to a skate park. I could maybe go to a mall, but lots of malls are cracking down on kids hanging out. Libraries don't let kids hang out. Where was I going to go?" The fact is, kids spend the majority of their waking hours in school. For this reason, as Pascoe acknowledges, much research on youth has "a very school-centric bias." And, partially for convenience, grade schools near prominent research universities are over-weighted in a great deal of research.

Knowing all this, as well as the strong liberal leanings of the geographic region in which she worked, led Pascoe to seek a school outside of the San Francisco Bay Area. Of course, as we also learned from Amy Schalet's work on teenage sexuality (in Chapter 1), getting access to a school is not always easy and often requires a bit of luck. As Pascoe explains, "Schools are such heavily surveyed sites at this point and are blamed for so many social ills that they don't necessarily want to let an outsider in."

To begin a relationship with her future research site, Pascoe offered free SAT tutoring and college application advice, both to gain the trust of potential research sites and "because I think when ethnographers ask people for favors, they should always try to respond or offer back whatever they can." Eventually, however, her success came down to an opportunity based on a confluence of factors far outside her control: Pascoe found a school led by a principal five years from retirement in a school district with a particular concern about understanding high school boys due to a recent sexual assault involving members of the football team.

in the halls

Once entering the site, the ethnographer faces a new environment filled with different norms and expectations. This can be thrilling, jarring, or both, and it requires adaptability. In some cases, this is a result of others in the site not knowing how to place you. Pascoe says, for example, "Early in the research, I showed up at this school site. I was wearing my standard research gear, which consisted of baggy cargo pants, which were in style at that time, a black fitted T-shirt . . . and I was wearing my little combat boots and a messenger bag slung sort of diagonally over my back. I was walking down the hallway, and I hear behind me this loud booming voice saying, 'Hey,

hey you there. Where's your hall pass?' I turned around, and it was the head school safety officer. I was like, 'Ah, I'm a researcher, I'm not a student.'"

This was the first of many moments of misrecognition: "The teachers often thought I was a new student, or every once in a while they'd think I was a substitute teacher. The students thought I was anybody from a new student to somebody's aunt to somebody's mom.... It really illustrated the way in which our audience really gives us our identity.... To be misread constantly is very psychologically jarring."

An ethnographer must also find ways to access the people of interest within the research site. As Pascoe quickly learned, some are more eager to share than others. In particular, the girls on the basketball team had little interest in her project. "They were super tough. They were all tall, and I'm very short, and they had this swagger. I would just watch them walk down the hallway and bang on lockers and ... torment boys by throwing things over their heads that boys couldn't catch because they were taller than them.... I just couldn't find a way to get in with them; they just wouldn't talk to me. I was sort of a nonperson for them."

As Pascoe's network in the school expanded, a cheerleader eventually helped her gain access to the female basketball players. The conversation came with further tests: "One of them, before she would talk to me, was like, 'So, have you ever gotten in a fight?' I haven't gotten in a fight. But, I managed to tell a story about this guy who stole my partner's bike, and I found him and pulled him off the bike. That is as close as I'd ever been to a fight, and I guess it made me look tough enough." Pascoe had to pass these tests to demonstrate that she was a safe person to talk to and that she wouldn't negatively judge the players' particular enactment of gender.

positionality

The amount of time spent in contact with people in the field and the relationships that come with this contact ensure that no researcher is just a "fly on the wall," taking observations in the laboratory of the social world. The researcher's identity shapes the field and is shaped by the field. To reflect on positionality is to consider your status in the field and how it may impact data.

For Pascoe, there were multiple layers to how her positionality played a role with the kids in her study: "my racial position, my particular gendered enactment, that I'm a woman—but at the time I was researching those kids, I didn't look like the typical women they knew. I had short hair, I wore baggy pants, that kind of thing. That I'm queer, which can certainly build bridges with some kids and really sort of drive a wedge into relationships with others."

For the skilled ethnographer, the question is how to recognize both the limitations and advantages of positionality. "Rather than trying to pretend that those differences don't matter, call attention to them. Be like, 'Huh, we have these differences, that's interesting. What do you think about that? Isn't it weird that I'm like sitting in your school? That's just super strange.' The worst mistake is to try to fake an identity and confidence, especially with youth, who seemingly have an unmatched ability to see through 'cool' facades. We all remember that teacher in high school who was like, 'I'm going to be cool just like you guys! I'm going to relive my high school days,' and you're like, 'Oh, wow, you're kind of a loser.'"

With transparency, these potential weaknesses can provoke conversation and become a strength. For instance, Pascoe would call attention to her age and gender: "I'd be like, 'Yeah, I'm totally different than some of the girls here, that's weird,' and we'd have a conversation about it."

the power of ethnography

Emotionally and physically challenging, ethnography has the potential to excite and thrill. That a method can be fun is too often lost in discussing (or justifying) research. Pascoe describes the rush of stepping into a world outside your own. This was most apparent when she could take a step back, go back to her familiar surroundings and have a sense of, "Whoa, I'm seeing really cool stuff, this is awesome, and I think that's a feeling that every researcher should have."

Ethnographers share the fun of providing insight into the worlds that many readers will never inhabit, by allowing the inhabitants to have their own voice. Many methods simply are unable to do this. Pascoe explains, "One of the things that we find with research, for instance with survey research, the voice is really the voice of the researcher. They have decided which categories are important and what questions shall be answered."

In contrast, an ethnographer hands over some of that power to the respondents: "You're like, 'You guys tell me what's important. You guys tell me what's happening in this particular social world.'" In the best-case scenario, Pascoe says, the ethnographer gives voice to folks generally unable to make pronouncements about the social world. "I think that is a really cool process, and a politically important process, to make sure that multiple voices are heard."

Precisely because of the embedded, messy nature of the ethnographic project, the researcher has access to an abundance of accounts that can draw the reader into the text in a way few other methods allow. Pascoe reflects, "The readers can feel it, they can smell it, they can hear it, and that is really important. We might not always remember the specific statistic or finding." But, Pascoe argues, insight into the subjective has the potential to be transformative: "That is one of the gifts that ethnographers have. We can humanize the process of inequality and, perhaps, get more people on board with pushing back against the forces that perpetuate inequality."

analyzing commercials

FEATURING MADISON VAN OORT AND
KYLE GREEN

E vidence for modern society's emphasis on the visual is not hard to find—billboards line the roads, television and computer screens are pervasive in homes and workspaces, and advertising covers an increasing amount of public and personal space. Considering this, it is not surprising that researchers use a number of visual methodologies. Discourse and semiotic analysis are two of the tools used to reveal the cultural messages and trends buried within visual, written, and vocal materials. Madison Van Oort and Kyle Green used a mix of these two popular approaches to analyze the advertisements broadcast during the 2010 Super Bowl. Through deep analysis of the symbols used and ideas drawn upon in the advertisements the two researchers reveal how companies constructed a sense of crisis to sell their products. In doing so, Van Oort and Green connect the representations of the current state of masculinity to broader anxieties about the recent economic recession and the empowerment of social minorities. The conversation illustrates the importance of embracing the subjectivity and creativity available in qualitative visual analysis. It also reveals how the same qualities that make some skeptical of the method can offer an accessibility that extends beyond the academic journal.

falling into a project and opportunity

Sometimes researchers find projects at unexpected times and in unexpected places. In this case, Green and his coauthor both watched the 2010 Super Bowl for the entertainment and spectacle. However, the next morning when they arrived at the office, they discovered that they had similar reactions to the commercials. "We both had a hunch that there was something different about this year. We were thinking specifically about the use of violence and how aggressive the commercials were against men." Neither was actively looking for a new project, but it seemed like there might be an important story to tell.

The next step was to figure out how to study the topic from a more sociological perspective. "Our research questions ended up being, What are some of the main narratives that are actually coming out in these 2010 Super Bowl commercials? How can we understand those narratives as situated within a particular social context or historical moment? And, importantly, how do these narratives compare to what's already been documented about Super Bowl commercials in years past?"

The confluence of events that led to the project reveals the importance of opportunity and luck—something rarely raised in discussions of methodological choices. Van Oort and Green happened to watch the same event and make a similar observation. They also shared an office in graduate school and chose to come to campus early the following Monday morning: "even if we waited a few days to come to the office, maybe that excitement would have been gone and it might not have happened."

the "super" cultural object

To Van Oort and Green, the Super Bowl offered a compelling context for studying commercials. The American national football title game claims over 110 million viewers every year and consistently breaks its own record. For the researchers, this alone "indicates that it's a particularly important cultural moment." As a result, Green explains, "the commercials cost a ridiculous amount, something like $3 or $4 million for every 30 seconds." Because advertisers don't intend to waste that money, "you know they're trying to pick up on the social currents of that year and find something that resonates with the public. We don't know what's going on behind the scenes, but we know something's going on, and they're trying their hardest."

The Super Bowl is also one of the few events where commercials are a key part of the event. Viewers are invited to vote on and rank the advertisements, and bloggers often provide real-time feedback as they air. Van Oort and Green suspected this was one of the few moments they could be sure people were actively watching the commercials, sometimes *instead* of the game itself. As Green points out, "The NFL itself is aware of this trend and now makes every commercial available online." For sociologists interested in advertising, there are few, if any, better events.

the method

To begin, Van Oort and Green constructed a data set of every Super Bowl commercial from 2008 to 2010. As they viewed each commercial, they paid particular attention to things like the company, the type of product, the characters portrayed (in terms of race, class, and gender), the dominant messages and themes, and the general strategies employed in each ad spot. "For instance, was the commercial violent or was it more humorous?" This quick quantitative overview provided a foundation for their analysis. It also gave both researchers confidence that "we weren't just cherry-picking commercials that had these bizarre themes and were actually just outliers," looking instead at real shifts over time.

Together, they decided on a blend of semiotic and discursive analysis to get a more in-depth reading of what story the commercials were telling in 2010. Van Oort explains, "We thought about our semiotic approach as something that reveals how meaning is attached to images. . . . A discursive approach is something that shifts the analysis to think about how the styles and the rhetoric that are employed actually relate to the power relations of that context." For example, "How might 'wearing pants' in a Dockers commercial relate to certain patriarchal myths about breadwinning and class identities? And, considering this particular historical moment, how might it also relate to broader changing relationships to work and economic security?"

After coding each commercial's every detail—from the body position to the clothing worn, hairstyles, and narrative arcs—Van Oort and Green then examined the relationships among the Super Bowl commercials to get a better sense of the larger narrative that was created. Understanding the "intertextuality," or ways that the meaning of one image (or

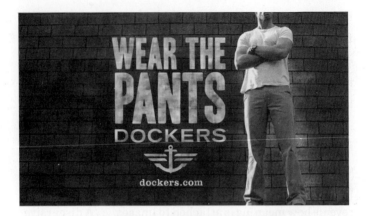

commercial) was in communication with the meaning of other images and commercials, formed a basis for their discursive analysis.

accepting limitations, embracing the subjective

As Van Oort is quick to point out, there are a number of available approaches to coding visual media. "Sociologists often are more likely to use something like content analysis, which is when the analyst seeks to discover common themes and patterns in a group of images or text. This often takes a quantitative turn: the goal here is greater replicability and a desire to answer a more clearly objective set of questions." In contrast, Van Oort and Green employed a qualitative form of analysis, "since we were not just looking at certain symbols and how frequently they appeared, but actually the social ramifications of them." Van Oort continues, "In other words, we weren't trying to prove that the crisis of masculinity is real through saying it appears x number of times." While coding and counting might make their approach seem more scientific and quantitative, "it would have been forcing the method onto the topic and it wouldn't have been the best way to get at the questions we wanted to ask."

Because the method is subjective and there is no right or wrong answer, it might seem easy for a skeptic to dismiss findings from this type of visual analysis. For this reason, depth of analysis, detailed description, demonstrations of rigor, and transparency are essential in convincing the reader of the value of the research. Tracing how themes travel across commercials is also a powerful way to convince the reader of the importance of the patterns—"it wasn't only Dockers that showed men happily wandering around in just their underwear. Right after that, we see a Career Builder commercial with the exact same thing. You can show this and say there seems to be some sort of message that's being repeated over and over."

Creative analysis also requires scholarly courage. "We both needed to be brave in the ideas that we were willing to try. We had to be willing to throw things out there that maybe seemed silly and to figure out whether or not those interpretations really stuck or were really meaningful." This willingness to travel down potential dead ends actually resulted in analytical serendipity: "You have these tiny moments that seem inconsequential but then you start reading across text, then you start looking at other commercials where this is happening and you realize there actually is something going on with that particular symbol that is worth unpacking."

Transparency and a willingness to reveal the position and views of the researcher is another way to build trust in analytic findings. Van Oort explains that they never claimed objectivity: "Instead, we came at it as two sociologists with somewhat similar, but also somewhat different, academic training and with eyes toward different kinds of signs and symbols. Kyle was interested and trained in more gender studies and theories of men and masculinity, whereas I was trained in queer theory and feminist studies." Green and Van Oort believe that pointing out these ideological differences and acknowledging their particular subjectivity gives "the reader a chance to work through the data and decide whether it's convincing or not. They can reject our argument, but they know where we came from and why we arrived at that conclusion."

making the ordinary strange

An unexpected benefit of their project was how easily it could import into the classroom. Van Oort explains, "Students can actually work through this with us or on their own. They can watch these commercials, they can come up with their own interpretations, and take ownership of what they are learning."

Because commercials are so accessible, they offer a great gateway for anyone to critically analyze popular culture—the classic sociological task of "making the ordinary strange" through guided deconstruction. As Green puts it, "Maybe you are watching a sports event with someone, and you point out a commercial and say, 'That's really different than what we saw last year,' or 'Why is there such an emphasis on men wearing pants?' or even 'What is the commercial trying to tell us?'" In other words, the accessibility and intuitiveness of the approach provide powerful political potential even outside the ivory tower.

comparative historical research

5

**FEATURING DAVID FITZGERALD AND
DAVID COOK-MARTÍN**

L
ike the previous chapter's researchers, David Fitz-
Gerald and David Cook-Martín wanted to "make the
strange familiar, and the familiar strange" in their
study of immigration policies, racism, and democratic socie-
ties. They elected to take a historical perspective, looking at
organizations, social movements, and social institutions over
time and in different places. For them, looking into the past
was powerful because it allowed them to understand historical trajectories and how "something that might seem natural
in one given setting can actually vary quite a bit across other
cases."

The authors knew that, over time, many countries in the
Western Hemisphere had set immigration policies to construct their populations—to "literally decide who would be
the insiders and who would be the kinds of people that would

not be allowed to enter and become part of these new nations." Given this, they wanted to study policies that sorted potential immigrants based on ethnicity, race, or national origin; which would help reveal the relationship between ethnic selection policies and governmental ideology. In their words, "We all know that the U.S. is a nation of immigrants, and we also know that there are lots of other countries that are nations of immigrants. In a nutshell, we wanted to explain a period of rising selection of immigrants by ethnic criteria, as well as the decline of those criteria, as it's often considered politically illegitimate to select immigrants based on their race."

Using archival data—in this case, written law—allowed them to bore down into the details and ask specific questions: How were these laws enacted and practiced? What were the social origins of these laws? How did the development of laws in one setting then affect the development of laws across countries and other settings?

Cook-Martín and FitzGerald quantitatively coded the immigration laws of 22 countries in the Western Hemisphere, written over 200 years. This first-ever comprehensive study of *all* Western immigration law traced legislation from each nation's independence, resulting in thousands of data points. This data set allowed the research team to map trends in formal immigration and nationality law. Then they dug deeper, conducting qualitative analyses of a collection of case studies from the bigger sample. The drill-down helped explain how and why patterns emerged and provided a fine-grain view of what was happening in key countries and international organizational fields.

what they learned

At its core, the study calls into question the widely held view that democracy and racism cannot, ultimately, coexist. The opposite was actually true: their analysis revealed a positive relationship between racist laws and a nation's purported goal of democracy. The data set of legal records between 1790 and 2010 shows that democracies were the first countries in the Americas to select immigrants by race, and undemocratic nations were the first to outlaw discrimination. But *why* would a nation that claims an ideally democratic society also write immigration laws designed to keep particular groups out? And how could the opposite also be true?

In their book *Culling the Masses*, the authors describe how the United States led the way in using legal means to exclude "inferior" ethnic groups. For example, Congress began passing nationality and immigration laws in the late 1700s that prevented Africans and Asians from becoming citizens, on the grounds that they were inherently incapable of self-government. Similar policies were soon adopted by the self-governing colonies and dominions of the British Empire, eventually spreading across Latin America. In contrast, political regimes in Chile, Uruguay, Paraguay, and Cuba *reversed* their discriminatory laws in the 1930s and 1940s, even as the United States enacted new measures.

FitzGerald and Cook-Martín say the project also reveals a gap between the law on the books and law as it's actually practiced. Even this came in paradoxical form, however. "People always assume that, secretly, governments are harsher than the law on the books would suggest. There are certainly many examples where that's true, but we found some really important examples of the law on the books being much, much harsher than the law in practice. So, whether or not it's going in one way or the other is an empirical question." Are the laws tough but rarely enforced? Or are the laws fairly lenient but an often-wielded weapon of nuisance or justification?

For a very long time, many have believed democracy depends on ideals of equality and fairness, which are incompatible with the notion of racial inferiority. But the data show that liberal democracies have been leaders in promoting racist policies and laggards in eliminating them. In the end, it took World War II *and* the Cold War to convince North American countries to reform their immigration and citizenship laws.

it was hard!

It should be clear by now that a project of this scope took a lot of work. The main problem was data. Even something as basic as the gross domestic product (GDP) measurement was almost impossible to get for the years prior to WWII in the majority of countries in the study. "You can't measure economic conditions systematically during this time period. That's something that's only available for a handful of the most developed countries like the U.S. and Canada. If you want to know, 'What was the GDP in Honduras in 1896?' Good luck! It doesn't exist."

The project was also a lengthier undertaking than the researchers expected. "We were, frankly, naive about how long that would take. We thought we would just write it all up and it would take maybe six months, and it took maybe six years. It was extremely difficult to figure out what the laws were and then to systematically code them for evidence of discrimination and for evidence of the use of different technologies of control."

FitzGerald and Cook-Martín also had to dig around to find the laws: Their study was conducted before large quantities of archival data had been digitized by libraries or historians, so it was an old-fashioned hunt for original source material. "It sometimes was overwhelming, to be honest. The idea of 'law' might seem straightforward enough, but something like immigration law appears in many different kinds of law. Sometimes the law is titled 'The Law of Immigration,' but sometimes immigration laws are in the Constitution. They might be in bilateral treaties, multilateral treaties, or court cases. There are many, many different kinds of law."

The authors were also constrained by a nation's past and present ability to devote resources to recordkeeping. "Just getting ahold of the laws was very difficult when it comes to governments of countries with less-developed state infrastructures. It's easy enough in the U.S. and Canada, but in a lot of Central American cases, getting that was really difficult. It was a combination of getting copies of government publications that would give all the new laws in these 'gazettes,' these daily government newspapers, or going to the archives. Often, it was easier to find these documents in a place like the New York Public Library than in those countries themselves."

This difficulty in sourcing data was among the most unexpected and fascinating aspects of the project. "It was some of the more exciting archival research that we did, to uncover some documents that have never been reported before, in neither the English nor Spanish literature. For example, there are some confidential restrictions on the Chinese in

Mexico that I found in the archives in Mexico City. Some of the documents were written partially in cipher [code]. I found other documents that decoded that and showed that it referred specifically to Chinese. David found some similar documents that have never been written about before in the archives in Argentina." Such puzzle-solving is one of the distinct difficulties and greatest joys of archival research.

lessons for the historical sociologist

Scraping together centuries-old data from many different countries means knowing that, inevitably, you're missing something. FitzGerald and Cook-Martín worried they would miss important dynamics and some of the more "fine-grained aspects of what may be going on in the case of each country. You also miss the stories from below, so to speak—you miss the way that people engaged some of these laws."

Yet, the authors' efforts to combine large-scale quantitative analysis with smaller-scale qualitative case studies allowed them to see *both* the law on the books and the law in action, and they were forced to think outside their own U.S.-centric position. "Showing these big trends is really important, in part because it makes us get away from our 'methodological nationalism,' which is naturally framing the project through the lens of whatever nation-state we happen to live in. We were getting beyond the blinders of just looking at the United States or thinking only about how U.S. policy developed in interaction with different countries."

It's a lot of work, but archival or historical projects can come with a big, unexpected payoff *and* they are replicable in other contexts. A researcher could, for instance, do a similar study by looking at institutions or organizations instead of the written law. This would mean "systematically looking at what a set of organizations have done, as well as doing some strategic case studies to elucidate the dynamic," which the authors argue "is a powerful combination. It requires a lot of space, but it gives the most complete [possible] understanding of a process" in rhetoric and practice.

part 2: explanatory and quantitative methods

Q uantitative research attempts to systematize the social world through numbers. These approaches transform observable data into units that can be analyzed statistically and mathematically. The resulting data offer powerful descriptives of the social world—revealing characteristics and generalizable patterns about a population or phenomenon of interest—and is a common first step in research. These results can then guide theoretical discussions, confirm or disconfirm hypotheses and prior research, and generate new questions.

Beyond description, quantitative approaches have the ability to *explain*, isolating and controlling targeted variables to understand relationships between them. In this section we have five authors, each demonstrating a different way of harnessing the descriptive and explanatory potential of the quantitative.

There are numerous approaches considered quantitative, as well as many intersections between quantitative research and other different approaches (such as qualitative, textual, and historical methods). Among the most fundamental quantitative methods is survey research, such as the U.S. Census or the General Social Survey. While the U.S. Census is a demographic project (attempting to count and classify the entire population), the General Social Survey is an example of a randomly selected subset of the population that is representative of the United States as a whole.

This methodological approach is appealing for a number of reasons. Researchers can make an educated guess as to how an entire population might think about an issue, for instance, without spending the resources to administer a survey to every single person who lives in a given country. By selecting an independent variable and statistically controlling for confounding variables, researchers can measure the effect of something like religious beliefs on political party affiliation, hypothesizing that the independent variable is correlated with or predicts the dependent variable. If surveys are conducted with the same group of respondents at different points in their lives, researchers can measure how people change over their life course.

While not exactly quantitative in terms of the data, experiments, both in field and laboratory methods, are often considered the gold standard of explanatory methods. Experimental research designs isolate a causal mechanism by creating matching groups, then changing a single variable in one of the groups to see what happens. In evaluating experiments, the focus is not on the number of cases but about the control of causal conditions. When done correctly, the social scientist is given the rare opportunity to claim with certainty that modifications to x do in fact lead to changes in y.

Quantitative researchers must take care in designing their projects, especially before they begin to collect or analyze data. In particular, the quality of the study depends on how well a researcher can truly measure various constructs in numerical terms. Because human behavior can be explained and interpreted in many ways, it's essential for quantitative researchers to carefully design their studies, write questions that accurately capture the social construct they are interested in, and collect data from research subjects who are representative of a broader group or population.

Understanding and evaluating quantitative projects requires the comprehension of a few key terms, especially generalizability, reliability, and validity. These are terms that will appear over and over in this section. *Generalizability* is the degree to which the results of a study based on a sample can be said to represent the results that would be obtained from the *entire* population. In simple terms, how well does the

General Social Survey or a Pew Research Survey match U.S. Census demographics? *Reliability* is the extent to which an instrument or variable is consistently measuring a construct. *Validity* refers to the accuracy of the variable or instrument itself. Even if a test is reliable across studies, it may not necessarily measure what it is supposed to measure. All of these are central not only to quantitative research, but also to *most* sociological research.

This section introduces five examples of very different forms of explanatory research. Some use quantitative data to explain or understand difficult-to-measure constructs, like inequality, aging, identity, or patterns of social problems. **Devah Pager**, for example, talks about conducting an experimental field audit to assess the effect of a criminal record and race on employment outcomes in real-world scenarios.

Instead of collecting new data, **Christopher Wildeman** uses an existing data set to ask new questions. By applying innovative methodological approaches, he transforms our understanding of child maltreatment by showing the cumulative life experience of maltreatment, instead of displaying these rates as impersonal statistics.

Deborah Carr uses a longitudinal design, collecting data from the same people at different points in time, to examine how people think about their personal goals and career trajectories. In her interview, she points to difficulties in retaining longitudinal study participants over the years.

The breadth and depth of quantitative or explanatory research are powerful. By collecting a large swath of data, researchers can understand and communicate shifts and trends and even, occasionally, make some predictions about future behavior. **Keith Hampton** offers an example of the explanatory power of large-scale content analysis by comparing videos taken of urban public space today and several decades ago. In doing so, he creates a pseudo-experiment to examine how cell phones and other technological innovations have changed the way people behave in public.

Andrew C. Billings's comparison of Twitter and traditional media through quantitative content analysis similarly employs structured rules to count various aspects of a particular media in the most reliable manner possible. Instead of relying on "the good eye," researchers follow a number of rules and procedures when selecting and coding the images and text in question. Here, the power of the method is not to find causality or an explanation for why something occurs, but to record and describe what exists, taking the initial steps toward classification and providing data on which others might build.

field effects in experimental audits

FEATURING DEVAH PAGER

iscrimination is extremely difficult to measure. Sociologists must heed social desirability bias, wherein respondents in surveys or interviews are unlikely to admit to discriminatory beliefs or even interpret their own actions as discriminatory.

So, when she wanted to study the effects of a criminal record and race on employment, Devah Pager (then a graduate student at the University of Wisconsin) decided to conduct an experimental field audit. In this case, that meant she actually hired young white and black men, matching them into pairs based on their looks and personality. These pairs went out into Milwaukee to apply for hundreds of real job openings. They switched off reporting a felony drug conviction on job applications so that Pager could isolate and measure the effect of criminal records on employment in practice. While experimental field audits yield real-world results and are relatively straightforward by design, they can be incredibly difficult to manage. Imagine, for example, the difference between a lab experiment, where researchers control the environment, and a field experiment conducted out in the world.

Before turning to Pager's work, we should take a moment to review some key terms associated with field experiments. First, they are often referred to as "audits," as the researcher aims to review and report on real-world behavior. Second, the actors hired to enact the experiment (in this case, apply for jobs) are referred to as "testers" (since they are conducting an experimental test) or "confederates" (since they are working with researchers to report something that's often not true about themselves in performing the experiment). The design is experimental because there is a control group to get a baseline percentage of employer callbacks (in this case, the tester without the record) and a treatment group (the tester who reports a felony on job applications in order to assess how much it decreases his chances of getting a job). And finally, there is an independent variable—the criminal record—predicting a dependent variable (an employer "callback").

Pager started with two main research questions. First, how much does a criminal record matter in hiring decisions in a low-wage labor market? And second, how does that effect differ depending on the applicant's race? For Pager, the appeal of an experiment was that she could account for all sorts of confounding characteristics that might skew her data. For instance, she knew from previous research that many people who end up in prison also have unstable work histories, substance abuse problems, and other difficulties that might make it hard to get a job. Pager also knew that looking at observational or survey data would only show a correlation between prison and employment. She was on the hunt for causality. By constructing identically qualified applicants and randomly assigning one member of the pair a fictitious criminal record, she could isolate her experiment's variables of interest.

None of the young men posing as job applicants actually had a criminal record. But, when a tester was assigned to the experimental condition, he would check the application box asking "Have you ever been convicted of a felony?" The testers would explain that they had been convicted of a drug felony, served 18 months in prison, and been released in the past month.

If the job application did not include a criminal record question, the tester would signal a record by saying that they had previously worked in a correctional facility and listing their parole officer as a reference. For each week of testing, Pager rotated which member of the tester pair presented evidence of the criminal record. If there were differences between the men who were posing as job applicants, Pager could control those effects by rotating their roles.

As hypothesized, criminal records had a big effect on employment outcomes. In Pager's words, "People with criminal records were about half as likely to receive a callback as equally qualified applicants with no record." She also found "some really striking findings related to race, so the effect of a criminal record was actually larger for black applicants. Black applicants with criminal records were about two-thirds less likely to receive a callback compared to a black applicant with no record. Whereas for white applicants, the difference was just half. So, a black applicant with a clean record fared no better than a white applicant who had just been released from prison. Essentially, the results suggested that being black in America today was viewed as essentially equivalent to having a felony conviction, at least for employers in these low-wage-level markets."

As expected, the study was difficult to manage. In comparison to lab experiments, field experiments are truly in the "field," so they are susceptible to many of the same difficult conditions that ethnographers face. For Pager, this meant a lot of work to minimize differences in testers' experiences at job sites. "The thing that makes it complicated to implement a study of this kind is just all of the little things that come up in the course of everyday fieldwork that can compromise the validity of the experimental design. And so I think the biggest challenge in conducting this research was just obsessing over all the little details. Like, 'Is the content of each resume exactly the same? What about how the testers are dressing? What's the script that we're using to present information? How might that shape or change the employer's response? What happens if the employer is available to talk to one tester but not available to talk to another tester? What happens if a tester gets lost in traffic?' You are trying to control everything so cleanly, but you are working in the real world, so lots of stuff is beyond your control."

An interesting side finding of this study was the effect of the experiment on the testers themselves. What did it feel like to go out into the real world and report a fictitious criminal record? To observe employer discrimination in a direct and quantifiable way? This was an unexpected and difficult example of positionality that's not typically discussed in explanatory work. "The human subjects review process [determining the ethics and outlining the process of a research project] thinks about 'subjects' in terms of the people that you are collecting data from (and in this case, that was the employers). But what was striking to me was that this project actually took a big toll on the testers themselves: the young men that were posing as ex-offenders. In particular for the young black men, they were enduring daily and repeated rejection from employers and kind of an immediate dismissal from these gatekeepers. That is really difficult to endure. I think that was something I hadn't anticipated in terms of the management and oversight of the project. The emotional toll that this work took on the testers was a really important thing to be mindful of."

In light of this emotional toll, Pager decided to change an original part of her study design when she replicated it in New York City. In Milwaukee, she had worked hard to keep the testers separated at all times. At first, she felt that it was important for the testers to report individually only to her so that they would not compare outcomes with one another and risk tainting her careful experimental design. But, the testers in the Milwaukee audit had to bear the psychological effects of racism and rejection without the support of peers. So, in the New York City study, which included a greater number of testers, she had the entire team come to work in the morning and return to the office together at the end of the workday. It proved to be an effective remedy to the emotional toll she saw Milwaukee testers face: "It generated an amazing camaraderie among the testers that they were all going through this experience together. They were able to debrief with one another and they could relate to each other's experiences in a way that I couldn't . . . since I wasn't out there pounding the pavement and encountering rejection over and over again. And I think that that was a much better environment for the testers to be working in than I would have expected. So that was definitely a learning process for me."

This type of positionality question is part of what makes experimental field audits such interesting and innovative studies. Because sociologists must endure the messiness of the social world, even the most controlled experiments require a great deal of attention to detail and anticipation of unexpected field effects. This makes for great empirical research, but as Pager cautions, "I would definitely remind [other scholars] that the devil is in the details and [to] keep in mind that [an audit study] sounds like a very simple approach, but that there are a lot of complexities to actually carrying it out effectively."

Audit studies are a fascinating hybrid of field research and experimental methods, helping to isolate the causal mechanisms behind social phenomena while still attending to the messiness of the real world. Amid the complexities, at their best, they are refreshingly simple in terms of design, analysis, and interpretation (and dissemination) of the findings. Rarely does a social science researcher have the ability to say with such certainty that x *leads to* y.

counting things in new ways

FEATURING CHRISTOPHER WILDEMAN

Numbers have allure. But the way we set up a study and decide how to count things have implications for how we understand the magnitude of a social problem. Christopher Wildeman has worked to develop better estimates of child abuse and neglect by applying demographic methodologies in his work. By changing the way he adds up the instances of this issue, Wildeman is able to better shape policy responses to and future studies of abuse.

how many kids will be maltreated?

Wildeman and his research team began at the beginning: What proportion of children will ever have a confirmed maltreatment case between birth and their 18th birthday? Then, how large are the sex differences and racial-ethnic disparities in this risk? To answer these questions, the researchers used the National Child Abuse and Neglect Data System's deidentified information on all children who came in contact with Child Protective Services (CPS) from 2004 until 2012. The data set provides information about who made the complaint, whether CPS confirmed the maltreatment, and what type of maltreatment the child suffered, alongside information on the child's age, race/ethnicity, and gender.

The traditional mode to estimate maltreatment was to use a simple annual rate. In fact, most statistics are based on an annual or daily rate of someone experiencing a specific event. For instance, researchers know that in 2012, about 0.8% of children had a confirmed maltreatment case. But, by thinking about maltreatment as a *cumulative* risk extending across multiple years, Wildeman and his team estimated that about 12% of children will experience confirmed maltreatment at some point before their 18th birthday. As Wildeman explains, "That's fully one-in-eight children, which is dramatically higher than I think anybody working in this area would have expected."

The technique Wildeman used is called "synthetic cohort life tables." Put simply, it asks, "Based on one year's data, what proportion of people could ever expect to experience an event at some point in their life, on the basis of these age-specific rates?" By only looking at the number of maltreatment cases per year, researchers had dramatically underestimated the total number of children who experience abuse or neglect. This approach is not new, but it is rarely utilized in sociology.

Wildeman found two other important patterns. First, while the cumulative risk of confirmed child maltreatment is very similar for boys and girls, the racial disparities are huge: "For African American children, between 20% and 25% will have a confirmed maltreatment case before their 18th birthday. Asian children have the lowest cumulative risks at about 4%, and white children have risks that are about 10%. So there are these pretty dramatic racial disparities, with African American children especially likely to experience this event."

Wildeman was particularly struck by how these findings relate to other social patterns in the United States. "The thing that is interesting for me, as someone who studies child welfare but also is a criminologist, is that about 25% of African American children will ever have their dad go to prison. We spend a tremendous amount of time as sociologists trying to figure out what's driving that risk and how it affects children. But the cumulative risk of having a confirmed maltreatment case for African American children is almost identical to that. Yet, in sociology, we've essentially just ignored this whole sort of subfield."

challenges

The work is important, not easy. The issues of dealing with an enormous data set compiled by a multitude of people and agencies meant it took Wildeman and his collaborator Natalia Emanuel 18 months to code the data in a coherent way. They had to match up data across years to ensure they were really getting the first confirmed case for a specific child.

Wildeman and his team also struggled with how to handle missing data on race and ethnicity. They had to make hard choices for how to code an increasingly multiracial U.S. population. For instance, "Kids who are half Hispanic and half Native American, for our analysis, end up predominantly getting lumped in as Native American. These sorts of textured distinctions, especially when you get down to the state level or the county level, end up being pretty consequential for how you think about a cumulative problem. We struggled with that a bit."

Another limitation is that for a data point to appear, CPS must have opted to launch a full investigation and made a ruling on whether maltreatment occurred. This important background can be lost in discussions of analytic results, especially when trying to figure out differences between race and gender. "We try to be very careful to say 'confirmed maltreatment' and to be clear about what's going on in these data. But the reality is that we don't know how big the racial disparities in actual maltreatment are. We only know how big the racial disparities in *CPS-confirmed* maltreatment are."

Wildeman's sociological training as an ethnographer and interviewer make him particularly aware of the limitations of large data sets. "One of the things that's hard with these data sets of 12 million observations is you can get to know the data really well relative to anybody else who's using the data, but you're never going to know the data as perfectly as you could with something where it's a smaller number of observations."

why does it matter?

This type of quantitative work is necessarily tedious and time-consuming. So what is the appeal? For Wildeman, the answer lies in the utility of the findings to improve social conditions for severely marginalized or hidden populations. "A lot of that work is based on feeling like I should have been doing something more useful with my life, like being a social worker. But, I would be a terrible social worker. It would be a total disaster. Part of what I try to do with this work is to think about my research subjects as being clients that I would want to see served well, and showing how much more of a social problem this is than we think it is."

Learning this data set also caused Wildeman to take a hard look at the system he was studying. Although quantitative data might sometimes feel abstracted or distant from the real world, he had the opposite experience. "It's hard to follow some of these kids through time in the data and not think that there's something pretty wrong with the way we're approaching things, or that we need to be thinking about doing a lot better than we are. That's not to say that caseworkers aren't doing a great job; I think caseworkers are doing the best job that they can. It's not to say that the Children's Bureau isn't doing everything they should be, because I have profound respect for them, too. But in a data set like this, you'll see the same kid experience the same type of maltreatment two, three, four, seven times within a given year, at the hands of the same person, but then the kid never ends up in foster care. I think that's been the sort of thing that's drawn me into the data a little bit more and made me think about what the point is."

Wildeman's study shows how taking a slightly different approach to quantitative research can yield more accurate results, significantly shifting our perception about a social problem's pervasiveness. Wildeman used these techniques to show that contact with the child welfare system is a consistent event in many, many children's lives—not the rare event it appeared in annual "snapshots." As a result, he says, "we can't ignore it anymore as sociologists."

the cost and benefits of longitudinal studies

FEATURING DEBORAH CARR

L ongitudinal studies provide a fascinating look into how people change over the course of their lives. In contrast to the more common cross-sectional approach, where data are collected across populations at a single point in time, a longitudinal approach adds time as a variable. By repeatedly interviewing or surveying the same individual at different moments and regular intervals, researchers learn how age, maturity, and shifting life circumstances change the ways we think and behave.

Deborah Carr takes this longitudinal approach in studying aging and goal attainment. Her work asks how people change their personal goals over time and what mental health effects might result from attaining—or not attaining— these goals. By using the Wisconsin Longitudinal Study, for example, Carr could look at what kids wanted when they were 17, and match that to their later accomplishments. As she explains, "You can't really look at people at just one point in time to understand what their lives are like. We really need to talk to people in multiple points over time so we can see how they change as they age. We also want to see how their experiences differ based on historical changes in the world that might be happening."

With Carr, we discussed what makes longitudinal studies so powerful in painting a complete picture of how people change over their lifetime. Of course, this approach comes with challenges. Long-term studies are difficult to manage and maintain. Researchers must carefully select their population and make sure survey questions are truly measuring the constructs they want to measure—because they're stuck with the sample and its design for a lifetime.

the study

The Wisconsin Longitudinal Study began in 1957, with every high school senior in the state completing a short survey about future plans. Questions included things like, "Are you going to go to college? What are you going to do?" In Carr's recollection, "Years later, a sociologist named Bill Sewell found this box of surveys and realized, 'Hey, this is really rich data. We should follow up with these high school students to see what happens to them.'"

Using the initial survey, research teams tracked down the original participants and reinterviewed them in 1975 when they were in their 30s; in 1994 when they were in their 50s; in 2004 when they were in their 60s; and most recently, again in their 70s. As Carr says, "We really have a complete life course history of this particular cohort."

Carr's study compared the participants' self-stated career goals in high school to what they were actually doing in their careers at ages 35 and 50. The question was, "What is the gap between what one wants and what one has?" The findings were rather unexpected. Men in their 30s who had a job of lower status than their high school selves hoped for showed depressive symptoms. Surprisingly, for women, Carr says, "It didn't matter what job they wanted at 17 or how it related to what they were doing at 35. It had no impact at all."

When comparing a person's age-17 goals to their accomplishments by age 50, Carr found another unexpected pattern: Among men, it didn't matter what they had attained relative to their age-35 goals. But, for women, there was now a huge effect: women who, at 50, had fallen short of the goals they had at 35 were much more depressed and had lower self-esteem. "There's this interesting puzzle: why did we find gender differences based on the age they were when they stated their goals?"

After conducting interviews, Carr realized that gender and historical context play an important role in self-perception. In the 1950s, men in their late teens often had high and lofty professional goals, while women had a narrower set of options: "Those weren't really goals that were heartfelt. Women knew they had three jobs at their disposal back in the '50s. Maybe they weren't particularly wed to the notion, but they said, 'I want to be a nurse, teacher, or social worker' because that was the only opportunity available for them."

When the women were interviewed at age 35 it was the 1970s. The world had changed, and women had a new array of opportunities available to them: "By their 30s, they got this new lease on life; they had these new career goals. If they had reached [those goals] by their 50s, they felt good about themselves." For men, if the goals stated at age 30 didn't pan out, they mostly passively stuck to what they were doing, no matter how dissatisfying, for the long haul. Overall, the study showed that goals are very much linked to historical social processes.

the challenges of longitudinal studies

Longitudinal studies suffer from selective attrition and high costs. That is, some people will drop out of the study over time, and attrition is not random. It is higher among less-educated people and those with fractured family lives, poor health, or early onset cognitive impairment. As a result, when the worst-off drop out, the remaining study participants will appear, on the whole, to be really "happy, healthy, smart, and wealthy." For those studying aging, it looks like, "Hey, people's health gets better as they get older—that's crazy!"

Further, just keeping track of people (especially for pre-Internet researchers) can be a costly endeavor. Carr and others at the Wisconsin Longitudinal Study employed a number of strategies for tracking down respondents. They used White Pages listings and asked respondents to give contact information for their family, friends, or neighbors. Researchers incentivize those who have dropped out of the study to be interviewed again by offering financial rewards or gifts.

But once someone is in a longitudinal study, you must avoid taking advantage of their generosity. "You can't drone on for two hours, or else they're going to hang up on you. You have to have questions that are clear, that are not leading. You have to have questions that do not trigger distress. They can't be questions that people will be offended by. If someone quits halfway through, then often you can't use any of your data because it's incomplete." The time and financial cost can rise rapidly as researchers work to recruit participants, track them down every ten years, and keep them in the study.

generalizability and validity

Finally, because longitudinal studies are time and cost intensive, researchers must carefully develop their sampling strategy. The goal is to construct a set of people who are generalizable to a larger population. Carr is aware of this limitation in the Wisconsin Longitudinal Study (WLS):

> Our sample is all high school grads, during a time period when not all people graduated high school. Our sample is Wisconsin, which is overwhelmingly white because, in the 1950s, African Americans and Native Americans in Wisconsin were far less likely to graduate high school. Whenever we write a paper with data from the Wisconsin Longitudinal Study, we know that someone's going to say, "Well, what does this tell us about blacks, what does this tell us about Hispanics, what does this tell us about people graduating high school in 1987 versus 1957?" There's always a tension between defending what you've done and being very honest. My sample at WLS cannot explain the experience of blacks and Latinos in California in the year 2012, nor should we try to do so. It would be dishonest and disingenuous. That's external validity.

Internal validity refers to whether the question really measures the construct the researchers are interested in, such as depression and mental health status. For Carr's study on goal attainment, she wondered, "Do people who reach their goals have better mental health? Well, you might have to consider the fact that people who reached their goals have more money. Or, people who reached their goals had happier childhoods and had happy, supportive parents who helped them reach their goals, and who also have the social support to ward off depression. You always have to think about competing hypotheses and then do the very best you can by carefully choosing reasonably sized groups of control variables to put into your analysis." When a researcher statistically controls for other life factors that might be driving results, they can isolate the effects in which they are most interested and make claims about causality. It's a tricky process.

benefits of longitudinal studies

Given the complexity of longitudinal surveys and the difficulty in tracking and retaining participants over time, Carr says survey researchers are extremely aware of the limitations of their methodology. But, she argues, the approach is essential to really understanding how lives unfold. If a researcher asks someone at age 65 to recall their life, they will likely reconstruct their past in a way that meshes with their current conditions, demonstrating a very powerful phenomenon called retrospective recall bias.

As Carr describes it,

If someone is depressed at 50 and you say, "Have you met your career goals?" they're going to say, "No, of course not." If someone's not depressed, they're going to say, "Yeah, I've been great at what I'm doing!" Your current mood taints all of your prior recollections. But, if you ask people their goals at 18, then you follow them up 20 and 30 years later, I can look at how they progress, and then see how those progressions affect their later mental health. You really are able to ascertain causal ordering, and you don't have to worry that someone's mucking up their perceptions due to their current mood. It's essential for aging researchers to have those multiple data points, to study whole lives as they are unfolding.

visual content analysis of urban space

FEATURING KEITH HAMPTON

Mobile phones are now ubiquitous, but we are just beginning to understand how they change our daily routines. In particular, there's a lot of chatter about how phones might negatively affect our ability to spend time in groups by encouraging people to sit alone in public spaces, tuned into their screens instead of one another. To empirically study this question, Keith Hampton and his research team compare video footage of public spaces taken 30 years ago and the very same spaces again today. For them, a *comparative, visual content analysis* was the best method to see the extent of any change in public interaction with the rise of the cell phone.

We came to this method as a result of our research questions. We had a question about how mobile phones might have been impacting relationships and interactions in public spaces, and we didn't have a good way of being able to compare that historically. The question was framed around our loneliness and isolation, and the value of participating in public spaces for what that does for things like exposure to diversity and deliberation. So, we had to select a method that would allow for a longitudinal comparison without having to stand on a street corner for 10, 20, or 30 years to try and get a sense of how it had changed.

To get at change over time, the researchers obtained film footage from a study conducted decades ago. Hampton recalls, "I remember from a class I took as an undergraduate watching William Holly Whyte's videos of interactions in small, urban public spaces and I had always dreamed of being able to try and find that footage and use it for comparison."

That meant Hampton had to find where the films were archived—no easy task. Eventually he found them warehoused in New Jersey in about 30 very large boxes. Watching the recordings, researchers realized they could refilm the same public spaces, replicating camera angles and locations. They selected four fixed-location films from the original footage: Chestnut Street in Philadelphia, Downtown Crossing in Boston, Bryant Park in New York City, and the steps of the Metropolitan Museum of Art in New York City.

replication

Though it sounds simple in theory, the actual task of recreating the footage was daunting. "We had to try and match the time of year, match the temperature of the filming from the originals, and match the angle of the camera so that we could include as much of the same frame from both time periods. That wasn't always possible to do. The original films were often taken from very unique vantage points that required access to different office buildings that were nearby, so we ended up purchasing a monopod, which is a tripod on a really big stick that went very high up in the air." The researchers also had to ensure the camera did not alter the social space. "We had to figure out how to secure it in a discreet way that didn't attract the attention of pedestrians or authorities."

The researchers let the cameras record over a number of different days to capture variation at each site, then began the process of comparing the old and new film footage. "We developed a coding scheme for what we were interested in observing, which in this case was individual people, whether they were in groups, whether they were male or female, whether they were using a mobile phone or not, and whether they were loitering in those spaces."

the findings

The analysis surprised the researchers in a number of ways. First, Hampton explained, people in the public spaces were no more likely to be alone than 30 years ago. Instead, they were more likely to be in groups, and these groups had more gender diversity. Specifically, "Men and women were walking together in ways that they didn't in the past, and in fact, there were many more women in public spaces today."

While the study was designed to learn about the impact of mobile phones, the researchers found that the gadgets played a surprisingly minimal role in life in public spaces. In fact, when people were in groups, they only actively used phones in public spaces less than 10% of the time. "So, the key finding really wasn't that mobile phones are having a big impact on public spaces. They weren't being used very often when people were in groups; they were being used when people were alone."

Hampton says his takeaway is that "a lot of research on new technologies is rather ahistorical, and really assumes that things were always so much better in the past; community was great, relationships were wonderful, everybody had access to public spaces, we were encountering diverse people there—and then today, things have just clearly gotten worse. But we really lack a kind of way of comparing the present to the past in a systematic way."

the unexpected challenges and benefits

Beyond the difficulties associated with filming, the biggest barrier for the project was time. In Hampton's terms, "It just took a ridiculous amount of time to code film. I mean, years and years. We wanted to do it systematically so that meant that you can't just let the film run and try and catch everything that's going on. You need to develop a sampling procedure. Our procedure was that we would sample every 15 seconds from the film, take a snapshot of that moment in time, code the content of that moment in time, and compare it to the same image from 30 years ago to see if the composition of people had changed as well."

Coding—and getting the coders to agree on that coding— was more demanding than Hampton anticipated. Ultimately, it took a researcher approximately 15 minutes to code every 5-second snapshot. The final data set contained 40 hours of film and nearly 150,000 individuals.

A time-intensive project is best done when structured around a clearly defined question so that time is not lost or wasted. "You really need to be very specific about what it is you're interested in before you get started. It's also true for survey research—you need to know which hypothesis connects with every single survey question that you're asking. It's the same for this kind of large-scale content analysis. There's no going back. Once you get started on this road and you're coding 150,000 people, you can't say halfway through, 'Oh, maybe I should code for yet another variable.' At that point, it's too late. So developing a coding scheme that's very precise and well-planned ahead of time is probably the single most important thing that you could do."

There are also limitations to the method in terms of generalizability and validity. Hampton's project encountered two main problems. The first was to sample public spaces that would make the study as generalizable as possible. The team knew that the original footage was not from randomly selected places and that local history and context have a lot of influence on public space. So, "the best we could do was to sample from a large number of cases and to try and pick places where we had a lot of original film. That's why we selected four different spaces. We felt that if we chose a greater number of places, as opposed to focusing heavily on just one place, it would give us greater variation, which might help our generalizability."

The second problem was internal validity in coding the film content. The team had to develop a way to ensure the coders were coding the same things in the same way. This meant a lot of training and regular check-ins to make sure all the researchers were still coding in the same way. The team would occasionally pause to code the same single frame of content, then assess the "inter-coder reliability" to see if they were doing the same thing. If they weren't, "then we all had to stop and talk about why we were seeing something different, and re-train on the moment to make sure that we were still going to code the same thing in the same way as we moved forward."

Innovative projects like this illustrate how big questions often require creative approaches. Hampton cites a fundamental strength of the project: "This is probably the only way to do a longitudinal study of public spaces. I mean, we can hang out at a public space for a month or maybe even a year, but doing that for two or three decades is just simply impossible."

real-time quantitative content analysis

FEATURING ANDREW BILLINGS

10

Our conversation with Andrew Billings illustrates the strengths, limitations, and methodological challenges of the quantitative approach to textual analysis. In this project, Billings, along with Lee Moskowitz, Coral Rae, and Natalie Brown-Devlin, examines the way traditional and social media responded to then–NBA player Jason Collins after he came out as gay. The benefits of using textual analysis include the ability to identify new patterns and trends and make comparisons across sites. Of course, the method also brings challenges, including the difficulty of coding accurately and consistently across media types.

For Billings, the method is all about revealing gaps: "I do gender research that examines gaps between how men are portrayed and how women are portrayed in the media. But, it can really be gaps between anything: between an actual percentage and a perceived percentage, between Americans and non-Americans." In this particular case, Billings and his collaborators looked at gaps between two different forms of media coverage: legacy media (represented by newspapers) and social media (represented by Twitter). Because this type of content analysis generates quantifiable data, the researchers can run tests that establish whether the gaps are meaningful as well as track the changes in media coverage over time.

studying in real time

Jason Collins's coming-out was widely discussed in the media and among the public. When Collins's carefully crafted announcement appeared in the pages of *Sports Illustrated*, it marked the first time a male athlete in one of the four major American sports (basketball, football, baseball, and hockey) had openly identified as gay while still an active player. For many, this was the last big hurdle for equality for LGBTQ athletes. And, while no one knew who was going to come out and when, rumors of a professional athlete, or group of athletes, coming out had been circulating for some time.

There was a limited window for Billings to be in the first wave of scholarly examinations once the announcement was made. Billings recounts, "I remember I had a friend on Facebook who posted that morning saying, 'Okay, the race is on for someone to get the first Jason Collins piece out there.' . . . There was a shelf life for this, so we needed to jump on that, and that actually caused us to look at some things in a different way." Content analysis offered a way to track the reaction that the announcement generated at a speed at which other methods could simply not compete. "Would I have loved to survey people right after that to see what their responses were? Yes. But at the time we didn't have any survey even started with the IRB. Without a human subject's approval, we were going to lose any window we had to get a real-time shot at discovering how people [were] responding to [Collins's coming-out]."

sampling and coding

Working across two types of media presented particular sampling and coding challenges unique to this particular study. There are a number of clear differences between how newspapers and tweets function, and each has to be addressed by the researcher. First is the overwhelming number of tweets. When studying newspaper coverage of an event, Billings said, "it's a bit easier. You have an aggregator (for us, that was the LexisNexis database) that gives us those stories, and then we can run keyword searches. If you do 'Jason Collins NBA,' you're pretty much going to get every story that you need" (in this case, Billings ended up with 364 newspaper articles).

In contrast, the research team collected over 40,000 tweets. "We decided there was no way we could look at each of those in a timely manner. We thought every fifth Tweet would be more appropriate, and so that sample became roughly 7,500 tweets. . . . That was enough to get overall trend lines, even with that short limitation of 140 characters."

The sample is further complicated by hashtags, used on Twitter to create easily accessed categories of messages. Sometimes hashtags helped the researchers identify and find a worthwhile tweet, but in other cases, they were superfluous or even deceptive. For instance, Billings described how a trending hashtag like #jasoncollins was used by corporations to promote their products by getting Twitter users to look at content they otherwise would not have stumbled upon.

The next challenge came in coding this massive amount of data. Coding is the essential step in any content analysis project, transforming an interesting collection of text into data ready for analysis. It seems counterintuitive that tweets would be more of a coding challenge than newspaper articles, but a newspaper article can contain multiple themes due to its length. In contrast, there is rarely space in 140 characters to introduce multiple ideas or perspectives.

Brevity can also add complications if the lack of context obscures the intent of the message. For example, "Coding for sarcasm can be really tricky, and that's the reason why we can't send it through a content analysis software program, because inevitably it's going to code things differently than the way they come out." Billings continues by explaining that for tweets like "I'm so glad we have people like Jason Collins sharing their bedroom habits with us," you have to make a judgment call about whether the writer is actually glad—or just being facetious. Here, the hashtags provided a great deal of value: "In the example I gave you, there might be a hashtag that says '#TMI,' for 'too much information.' At that point, it becomes very easy to code. People on a social media platform are going to make sure that they've given some little tip of the hat to what their core intent was."

After the coding was complete, Billings and his collaborators compared their counts across the mediums. They soon learned that the silences between platforms spoke loudest. As they analyzed their data, they looked not only for frames of selection and emphasis (what the tweets or articles were saying), but also for frames of exclusion (what they were not saying): "it is not just about what's there, it is about what's not there."

Through comparison across the two mediums, it became apparent that social media response quickly deviated from mainstream coverage. As the story evolved over the course of several days, Twitter became increasingly less reflective of the mainstream media framing. By the end of the week, over half of the tweets contained none of the frames the researchers identified in the newspaper coverage. While newspapers continued to focus on how the event was a watershed moment, make comparisons to other cases, and highlight celebrity support, Twitter users were able to introduce a number of themes, including civil rights. And, even though Twitter deviated freely from traditional media, newspaper stories continued to rely heavily on Twitter to report on the public reaction to an NBA player's open sexuality.

limitations

Because their emphasis was on finding "the gaps" between how two mediums covered the same story, Billings and his collaborators cannot easily generalize their findings to other instances of athletes coming out. Jason Collins is a single case without real comparison. "Certainly, we have plenty of research and plenty of access to different 'coming out' stories, but the bottom line is, Jason Collins's story is incredibly unique. That's why it resonated with the masses." Even if Collins had been a football or baseball player, the story may have looked very different. Additionally, his gender, race, and even his physical characteristics shaped public and media responses: "There are all sorts of aspects of him that make it very hard to apply to any other future case that may come."

Twitter itself presents an important data limitation. Billings explains that only 9% of Americans are active on Twitter, and within Twitter itself, 90% of the tweets are authored by just 10% of the user population. This means that tweets are coming from a very small segment of the population that is actively interested in the story. So, while patterns exist, they can't paint a full picture.

the takeaway

Billings cites this study as an example of using different media to explore a single research question. By using Twitter and newspaper articles, Billings reveals how these media's messages correlate and diverge. This better reflects a world where newspaper articles cite social media posts and people find their long-form journalism through links on social media.

Our discussion with Billings also shows the value of knowing what a method is and is not. While quantitative content analysis lacks the depth of some other methodological approaches and has a limited ability to answer "why," it is a quick and powerful method for providing the description and comparison necessary to answer "what"—an excellent and overlooked starting point.

As Billings explains, "Before we figure out why something exists, or what the effects are of something existing, we have to know what exists." He continues that too often researchers want to jump to step four or five, and that "many times what we think is going on, isn't what's actually going on." In sum, there are many possibilities ahead if researchers continue to pair descriptive approaches with integrated media studies. And, perhaps most exciting for those interested in the method, as Billings demonstrates with his use of Twitter, the power and speed of the method only increases with technological innovation.

part 3: mixed methods

Mixed methods research takes advantage of multiple ways to explore a phenomenon or address a research problem. By blending and combining approaches, researchers play off the strengths and limitations of each. While some use different methods to look at different aspects of related phenomena, others elect to look at the same question with different tools. Mixed methods research, then, has the ability to bring together the exploratory, the descriptive, and the interpretive. Mixed methods researchers also often draw on both quantitative and qualitative data. All together, the mixture of methods can allow researchers to "triangulate" data sources and thus enhance validity or see a topic from different angles and arrive at richer conclusions.

As a research approach, mixed methods is a set of principles and procedures put in place to answer a question or achieve a particular analytic interest not possible through a single method. As a research strategy, mixed methods describes the procedures put in place to achieve this goal, such as the use of ethnography to contextualize content analysis or to complement a survey with interviews.

There is also methodological flexibility in this approach—sample sizes and data collection techniques can be adjusted vis-à-vis the other methodological tools used in the same study. Interpretation of the data occurs in relation to multiple sources of collection, it is continual, and it can influence later stages of the research process.

In sum, mixed methods are used to overcome the limitations of a single design, to explain and interpret, to explore a theoretical perspective, to complement the strengths of a traditional research model, or to overcome the weaknesses of an approach. Mixed methods research can also be useful in deconstructing unexpected results and in bolstering or explaining both qualitative and quantitative results.

At first glance, a multiple methods approach seems particularly appealing; however, combining multiple approaches can become the equivalent of conducting multiple projects all at once. This can be time-consuming, expensive, and logistically difficult. Each method might raise new questions and ideas, which can lead to a study continually growing in size and scope, pulling the project in multiple directions. Employing multiple methodologies also requires technical proficiency and training that raises age-old debates about the advantages of mastering a specific area of expertise versus achieving proficiency across a spectrum of methodological skills and bodies of knowledge.

Our interviews with three mixed methodologists illuminate this melding process and show distinct uses of mixed methods from interdisciplinary collaboration to using multiple sources to answer a big sociological question or using multiple methods to track a single cultural phenomenon.

Helen B. Marrow joins a diverse team of researchers from multiple disciplines to construct a three-part study of immigrant-native relations in the United States. By using survey data, follow-up interview data, and observational data, the team discovered a host of unexpected outcomes regarding the effects of intergroup contact and trust. They also demonstrate how collaboration can overcome some of the challenges of mixed methods research.

Vincent Roscigno uses historical archives, correspondence, and qualitative and quantitative analyses to understand state power for a project on the Wounded Knee Massacre. His unique project takes multiple approaches to more roundly answer a sociological question.

Matthew Hughey studies the "white savior" trope in popular films using three different data sources: the films themselves, film critic reviews, and audience reception. By employing multiple methods, Hughey is able to follow the production, distribution, and consumption of a single cultural object.

collaborative research and question-driven methods

11

FEATURING HELEN B. MARROW

Some topics are simply too big to research effectively with a single methodology, as a lone researcher, or even from within the confines of a single discipline. Still, as each additional layer of complexity and intellectual tradition adds greater potential for understanding, it brings with it greater potential for miscommunication and error.

Marrow's work helps us understand the value of conducting research as part of a larger interdisciplinary team and see some of the methodological challenges of collaboration. She also offers valuable reflections on how mixing methods can increase confidence of validity and, somewhat counterintuitively, make each of the individual methods used that much more convincing.

the study

Sociologists Helen Marrow and Dina Okamoto came together with social psychologist Linda Tropp and political scientist Michael Jones-Correa around a shared interest in immigration and race relations. The topic is increasingly salient as immigration continues to rise within the United States, thereby increasing contact between groups that had little previous experience with each other. Marrow and her team "felt that the consequences of contact within this contemporary context of ethnic diversity, particularly for key social outcomes like trust and civic engagement, were still far from clear."

Some scholars have suggested that a rise in ethnic diversity leads to less community and civic engagement, while others argue that increasing diversity promotes the reinvigoration and enrichment of American civic life. Additionally, Marrow explains, "Previous work on intergroup contact still rests largely on a black/white paradigm in the American context." Her research team aimed to broaden the conversation to consider multigroup contact, moving beyond race or socioeconomic status, to also consider national origin, language, accent, religion, skin color, citizenship status, and so on. While the research team came from different disciplinary backgrounds, they were united by their shared interest in investigating where and how contact occurs between immigrant and native groups—and how that contact predicts civic engagement.

the methodological approach

Marrow and her team decided on a tripartite design for the project—meaning they would employ three methodological approaches, each building upon the type of data they were able to access through the previous approach. In this case, they had survey data, follow-up interview data, and observational data: "Ultimately, we chose to proceed with a survey as our primary tool in the first stage of the process. We felt that a randomized survey would end up giving us the most leverage to test several of the key aspects of the theoretical model and the hypotheses about relationships between immigrant-native contact, threat, trust, civic engagement, and so forth."

To test out their research design, they ran a pilot study in Philadelphia. The following summer, the group conducted a full survey in Philadelphia as well as Atlanta. These research sites were chosen for theoretical and demographic reasons: "We wanted two places where black/white relations have a significant presence in history, but we also needed places where there was a sizeable enough contemporary immigrant stream from both of the national origin groups that we had pulled from."

In the third summer, the group conducted semistructured interviews with a subset of their survey respondents. Graduate research assistants also conducted "brief time-limited observations" of public spaces that research participants had identified as sites of intergroup contact. While the research team did not have time for the level of immersion necessary for a full-scale ethnography, the field observations provided first-hand data on how the groups being researched were interacting, thereby "privileging the survey and the interview data and trying to tie some of these observations back to that data."

Marrow is quick to clarify that the topic and questions drove the methods, rather than the other way around: "These are huge issues. We wanted to make sure that we were focusing on a topic and asking questions about a topic that we were excited about first, and only then developing out the research methods and a project design that would help us answer our questions." Marrow continues, "I don't think that there's a right method or a wrong method, or a strong one or a weaker one. I, for example, have the strongest specialty in qualitative interviewing, but ultimately I think that your method should be suited to your question and your topic, not necessarily vice versa."

Because of the scale and complexity of the project, there was little flexibility to change course once the researchers started down a particular path. For this reason, it was important that each group of researchers and the team as a whole thought through and justified each methodological decision. For example, Marrow explains that the focus on native whites, native blacks, Mexican immigrants, and South Asian Indian immigrants was carefully determined. "One of them obviously represents the typical native-majority dominant racial group (that's native whites), another represents a native minority and subordinate racial group that's typically been studied in the literature (native blacks). One represents today's quintessential low-status immigrant laborer group (the Mexican immigrants), and the other, at least if you look at today, in the broad view, represents the quintessential highly skilled immigrant professional group (Indian immigrants)."

challenges

Collaborating has many advantages, but it requires work and ongoing communication and exchange among researchers. This is especially true when working across multiple disciplines and institutions and managing a team of 20–25 research assistants. As Marrow reflects, "The benefits are certainly enormous, and I think they outweigh the drawbacks, but this kind of collaboration and the size of the project often means that things move slowly, or that no one person has complete control of a process at any time or control of the timing of our work schedule." As a result, no matter how good the communication is, sometimes things happen in the wrong order, sometimes mistakes are made, and sometimes work needs to be redone. Of course, "some of those things happen in sole-authored projects of a smaller scale, but some of the things, they just grow and there are more of them."

The challenges of sampling are also magnified with scope. "You read a lot of articles here and there, '*This* is how we sample,' '*This* is how we do things.' What you don't read in them are all the things that kind of went wrong or that were worked around.... There are lots of things that go wrong. They don't make your project weaker, but you've got to figure out how to deal with them."

The team found some groups were harder to contact or were less likely to participate, which made efforts to fill quota categories difficult. However, as Marrow expertly demonstrates, sometimes the challenges tell an important story and can be incorporated into the analysis. For instance, it was especially clear that the Mexican immigrant group was the most distrustful, even when her team made use of Spanish-language coethnic and coracial interviewers. Marrow reflects, "There really is something about the low levels of trust that are showing up among Mexicans that are affecting even the interview completion process, and we have to bring that into the analysis of the Mexican immigrant experience today."

validity and convincing the skeptics

Marrow's team shows some of the key advantages of conducting a multimethod study. First, they had increased confidence in the internal validity of their work as a result of employing multiple methods. As Marrow put it, this means being confident that "the data you're picking up are true representations of what you're actually trying to capture and measure among whom you're trying to capture and measure it with." Here, the research is not as concerned with whether the data is applicable (or externally valid) beyond the people or places included in the study. For Marrow, "I think it's really important to make sure you always have internal validity; if you have external validity on top of it, that's great, but you have to have internal validity." While it is impossible in social science to know with 100% certainty that you have collected internally valid data, the multiple methods help. "You can try to triangulate around your topic and your question with different methods."

A second advantage of mixing methods that Marrow cites is perhaps less intuitive: "When you speak to people who privilege one type of data over another—and that is almost always people who privilege quantitative data over qualitative data—they actually listen to you!" Marrow continues, "I have spent my entire career trying to defend qualitative methods; the epistemology of it, the purpose of it, the usefulness of it, and it absolutely infuriates me that I keep having to do it." However, in this project, the quantitative data became a sort of Trojan horse helping to carry in the qualitative data. "It can actually be a way to really play up the strengths of qualitative methods. For someone, let's say, who privileges quantitative measures over qualitative ones, showing them sometimes how much better an interview can answer something than a survey can answer it is pretty powerful."

new ways of knowing

In collaborative, interdisciplinary research, scholars end up learning new ways to study the social world. This was important to Marrow: "I feel like I've learned so much in the past four years working on this project. I came in with an expertise in qualitative interviewing and somewhat in observing." She continues, "I've actually learned how to look at it through a survey and quantitative analysis. I've learned how to negotiate with and field a survey. I've learned about cell phone survey sampling, targeted geographic survey sampling. I've learned how to put a budget together. I've learned about hiring and training and establishing relationships with the research assistants."

The learning also results from crossing disciplinary boundaries: "I learned how psychology and political science think about intergroup contact differently than sociologists do. A lot of fierce debate about whether more contact between groups reduces prejudice and produces positive outcomes or whether it leads to greater feelings of threat and more negative outcomes has to do with the fact that the different disciplines are operationalizing and measuring 'contact' differently. Psychologists think about contact as direct, face-to-face contact, but often in sociology and political science, we're thinking of contact at a broader, more macro-level. We're thinking about: what is the racial or economic composition of your neighborhood?"

Bringing these perspectives together serves to strengthen the project. "It turns out if you just kind of learn from each other's disciplines you realize that there are these multiple ways to conceptualize and measure these things that you're interested in. You end up with a much more sophisticated picture and you just learn a lot more."

mixing methods to see bigger pictures

FEATURING VINCENT ROSCIGNO

When Vincent Roscigno and his team of researchers wanted to answer a big sociological question, they quickly realized their best strategy was to blend a multitude of methodological approaches. That way, they could go beyond identifying relationships to exploring the how, the why, and the "so what" of these relationships.

Their project centered on a single historical event, the Massacre at Wounded Knee. But the larger question driving the work was, "How do powerful actors justify the 'doing' of inequality?"

As Roscigno explains, "mixed methods" does not simply mean using a bunch of different methods. The actual mixing and melding becomes an art or a craft within sociology: "the blending of different types of research methodology to get at different parts of the same question. A multimethod approach is a creative endeavor: mixing methods in such a way that gives you a fuller sense of relationships that exist in the social world."

Most scientific thinking revolves around singular relationships or isolates the effect of one variable on a different variable. The mixed methods researcher is searching, instead, for the forces that might cause this relationship. As Roscigno puts it, "We have a treasure trove of qualitative, historical, ethnographic, and archival methods that can fill in that black box; that can explain *why* there's a relationship between x and y, not just *if* there is a relationship."

the wounded knee project

Roscigno began with a foundational interest in how persistent patterns of inequality are reproduced over time. Throughout his various research projects, Roscigno began to be intrigued by a related question: how do elites (whether individuals or institutions, such as local, state, and federal governments) justify and legitimize the "doing" of inequality or taking violence against a population? For him, studying the perpetrators of violence at the Wounded Knee Massacre was an intriguing and useful way in, partially because sociologists had never really dealt with it effectively and because it was a tremendously important historical moment. "I thought, 'Hey, why not? Why not me? Let me take a shot.'" In this case, settling on the case was a big part of the research process itself.

"We can think about this question as being relevant across all historical time: How did the pharaohs justify doing violence? How do kings justify doing violence? How do democratic governments justify doing violence or inequality relative to their own populations? So, the question is very broad, even though this specific article takes the Wounded Knee Massacre of the Sioux in 1890 as the case in point," Roscigno says.

The researchers began with archival research in the U.S. National Archive's collection of correspondence between government actors, military actors, and Office of Indian Affairs officials. They received a set of microfilm reels that contained all letter correspondence pertaining to the Sioux during this time period. The team read and coded these correspondences. As they worked, Roscigno says, "We mapped the [references to] Ghost Dance rituals and realized the historical materials confirmed that large numbers of Sioux engaged in this particular dance. So, I really wondered to myself: Was there a linkage between this spiritual practice and how the government responded?"

"We found that, sure enough, the federal government and the Office of Indian Affairs vilified the Sioux in various ways just prior to the massacre by suggesting that they were savage and immoral, and that they were not assimilating quick enough to the American way of doing things. This thing they were participating in called the 'Ghost Dance' was sort of a conduit by which the government was making these claims."

Through reading secondary historical research, performing geographic analyses of the Ghost Dance ritual, and coding the letters, the researchers were able to map out how the rituals were framed as Sioux resistance to American culture— and used to justify violence against the Sioux people.

mixing the methods

Having established this relationship, the team began to investigate the context and background. They noticed in their quantitative analyses that the military correspondence did not predict the massacre in the same way other governmental correspondence did: The military wasn't "vilifying the Sioux according to these documents. That really required us to take a step back and dive back into the qualitative data and figure out what was going on. As it turned out, the military, really quite strikingly, almost took the side of the Sioux against the federal government and Office of Indian Affairs. The military made quite explicit claims that they thought the major problem with Sioux assimilation was that the government itself violated its own treaties with the Sioux. They were not delivering needed and agreed upon rations to the Sioux, and that this is where some of the Sioux agitation was coming from."

Roscigno credits the findings to using mixed methods. "We would have never been able to come to that conclusion had we relied solely on the regression analyses: The regression analyses just told us that the military did not vilify the Sioux relative to federal actors. It really required a reimmersion into the qualitative material to figure out what was going on."

The research team was further able to conclude that this "dual dynamic" of amplification of the Ghost Dance ritual and vilification of the Sioux people who performed it was only one example of how government and institutional leaders reproduce patterns of inequality. Roscigno has spotted similar patterns across his other studies of inequality, for instance in workplace discrimination by race, gender, and age. "I suspect that amplification and vilification happen all the time. I essentially see organizational elites do the same thing to justify discriminatory actions. On the one hand, they vilify the victims of the inequality, but then they amplify something that is sort of culturally appealing to most audiences."

In this case, the mixing of methods involved bringing together a variety of novel approaches. First, they had to navigate using an old technology, ultimately opting to digitize the microfilm provided by the Archives, then still had trouble reading the faded, handwritten cursive of the 1800s. Then they had to figure out how to systematically code the correspondence into usable sociological data: "One way to do that is to create a coding device that lays out the themes of interest that you're looking for in a given document, and then having yourself and your collaborators go through these letters and systematically code one so you can compare and look for patterns between them."

This is a tricky and cumbersome task. Roscigno warns that even after creating what seems like an appropriate coding device, "you'll say, 'Let's go, let's start coding!' And you get three cases in and you go, 'This coding device is not working. There are themes here that I have to add, or I'm coding every single device exactly the same on this one so we really don't need that one.'" This pattern of testing and retesting is not unique to coding. Roscigno compares the process to survey work and refining questions. When working with multiple coders, researchers must also take into consideration issues of reliability and potential biases across coders, all of which must, too, be checked and rechecked.

The main thing, says Roscigno, is to "stay true to your question, and not lose sight of what that question is. Try to imagine what the ideal data would be, and then see if you could find it. Spend time digging around. Make sure it's not there before you sort of give up on it."

why mixed methods

Trained in quantitative methods, Roscigno "came out of graduate school running powerful statistical models so I can come away with confidence going, 'Yep, there is a relationship between x and y, or $x1, x2, x3$, and y.' But I was never completely confident on the validity side. I was unsure as to whether the variables I was using were really capturing exactly what I thought they were capturing, or I was uncertain about what the relationship was, or how or why there was a relationship there."

That search for validity pushed Roscigno to become a multi-methods researcher: "I think that various types of qualitative approaches can both give us confidence in the validity of the variables we tend to choose, as well as bolstering confidence in our interpretation of what that relationship is exactly." Another appeal of multimethodological research was its ability to "reveal aspects of social structure and social relations that a singular approach could not get at. I think it's rich."

Roscigno's practical advice is, "Don't be practical! Be creative, and think really big at first. I'm a believer that there's a lot of data out there, you just have to find it, even if you might have to do the grunt work and the cleaning work to do it." He also warns researchers "never to lose sight of the theoretical question and its underlying complexity, especially when you're complementing data and methods."

Mixed methodologists must be "ruthless in the pursuit of that data before you settle for easy, prepackaged data sets. I think some of the best, most exciting sociology comes out of that relentlessness. Somebody who's willing to dig around, to find data or multiple sources of data that suit the complexity of the theoretical question they're asking and then is willing to actually get their hands dirty and do the work; to gather that data, to clean that data, and to put it in a form that is amenable to sociological analysis."

The abundance of available methods makes this a promising period for mixed methods sociology. Roscigno reflects, "It's powerful. It puts a human face on the processes that we sometimes talk about in the abstract. It puts a human face on the authors that we're talking about and gives me, I think, correspondingly, a sense of confidence in understanding."

But none of this is easy: "It's challenging. It takes time. It requires confidence that you can find the types of data and integrate the types of methods you need. It really does require a creative mind with some energy behind it to be rigorous and relentless. I would encourage people to maintain a commitment to creative, rigorous thinking in constructing their projects. I think it's worth it and sociology needs much more of it."

following the circuits of culture

FEATURING MATTHEW HUGHEY

C ultural sociologists often have to decide whether they want to study the production, distribution, or consumption of the cultural object in question—what Stuart Hall famously called the "circuit of culture." That decision helps determine the types of questions to ask, the methodology to employ, the data to gather, and the claims that will be made.

In his analysis of race and film, Matthew Hughey elects to examine all three aspects of the circuit of culture by employing multiple methods. Here, Hughey helps us understand the challenges of his "tripartite methodological approach," the way that the question and topic determine the appropriate method, and the benefits of following a film genre along the circuit of culture.

the study

Hughey's research is on what he terms the "white savior film"—the feature-length Hollywood films that feature a struggling group or person from a lower- or working-class, urban, or "exotic," nonwhite background. In the course of the movie, a white person, "the 'savior' enters that setting and through his or her sacrifices as a teacher, mentor, lawyer, military hero, aspiring writer, or even wanna-be Native American warrior, is able to physically save or at least morally redeem a nonwhite person or community of folks of color by film's end." Hughey is certainly not the first to take interest in films about a white protagonist showing poor people of color the light, but previous studies have tended to isolate a single film for study. For his part, Hughey says he set out to "examine the most popular 50 white savior films over the last 25 years or so in order to look for their common denominators, something no one else had done."

Hughey also wanted to look at the role of film critics, placing them within historical and social contexts: "Sociologists have only recently taken seriously the role of gatekeepers when analyzing how and why certain cultural products become successful, or why they don't. I wanted to examine how film reviewers are influenced by the racial climate in which they make their supposedly individual appraisals." Hughey says, "After all, about one third of filmgoers report choosing the film they see based upon reading favorable reviews."

Finally, Hughey wanted insight into the consumption of culture: "I wanted to know about how people actually interpret these films, both consciously and unconsciously." Altogether, Hughey's research brings together content analysis of film, discourse analysis of film critics, framed analyses about perceptions of racial conflict, and in-depth interviewing and focus group studies of audience receptions of these films. In this way, he can study "the production, the distribution, and the consumption side of the media, without valorizing one at the expense of another."

Hughey's guiding research questions and methodologies emerged from this desire to get at the bigger picture: "First, I wanted to know, how do these films reproduce or contest dominant racial structures of meaning? Second, how did the variations in race relations relate to the viewers' interpretations of these films? And, third, how do audiences make meaning of these films?" To answer his questions, Hughey worked with five different data sets: contents analysis of 50 white savior films from 1987 to 2011, critic reviews of the 50 films (taken from the Movie Review Query Engine), 83 interviews with audience members, 8 additional focus groups with the same respondents, and a content analysis of *The New York Times'* coverage of racial conflicts.

the challenges

Taking multiple methodological approaches can be tough for a researcher. Leading this sort of project requires a deft ability to employ multiple methodologies and keep track of various types of data sets—as well as the confidence to move outside the narrow confines of one's expertise. This is a daunting task, particularly in the study of film and media, which is dominated by analyses of a single object or a single part of the circuit of culture. "When a sociologist of the media actually moves away from the text itself and begins to encounter people, who are sloppy creatures, they then run the risk of a disconnect between what the sociologist says the media means and then what the audience says it means." Moving from cultural object to gatekeeper to audience can place the researcher in a precarious position. "For example, what if I evaluate a film and find it particularly rife with white supremacist themes, but then I find that people of color seem to love the film? Do I then tread the dangerous road of saying that those people are all cultural dupes and are looking at the film with kind of rose-colored, false-consciousness glasses or do I risk my professional credibility and backtrack on my prior evaluation of the film? There's no easy answer . . . so I think a lot of people simply avoid looking at media reception."

Hughey is particularly well suited for this type of study, however. A self-described "methodologically promiscuous sociologist," he dabbles in different methodologies and data sources depending on which types of questions he wants to answer. Best known as an ethnographer, Hughey is quick to adapt his approach. "If I wanted to know something about the ways that audience members develop, nurture, and deconstruct, let's say in their everyday lived experiences, a film genre such as the 'white savior' film, that type of analysis would call for a kind of ethnographic strategy in which I would need to embed myself with a community of avid filmgoers." Since, for this study, Hughey was interested in "what kinds of demographic and interactive settings influenced how audiences made meaning of just a handful of these films, then interviews and comparisons between focus groups fit the bill for my question."

Employing multiple methods as a lone researcher means the same person must be familiar with each method. "This was really my first use of focus group methodology. And so I really had to take myself back to school and read up on what is an immense and longstanding sociological method that's been somewhat marginalized in recent years. So, I played to my strengths, but I also went out on a limb in this study."

the benefits

Both the challenges and the benefits of Hughey's approach are evident. This work fills a void through sitting at the intersection of the sociology of race and ethnicity and the sociology of the media and pop culture. As Hughey puts it, "In a world that's becoming simultaneously more media-saturated and also more racially confusing—that is, we have this post-racial discourse but very racialized realities . . . people seem to want to look at multiple angles of a particular phenomenon. I think this book that examines so many different aspects of this racialized media genre will appeal widely."

As illustrated by Van Oort and Green's study of Super Bowl commercials in Chapter 4, the consumer's interpretation of the object of study often remains a black box. By conducting focus groups, Hughey is able to illustrate how their own racial status directly influenced participants' interpretation of a white savior film. He also found that participating in a group discussion both solidified and guided an individual participant's interpretation. Taken together, these two repeated observations demonstrate how the identity of the participant and social context of the viewing can override the message of the film.

It is rare for a cultural study to examine production, gatekeeping, and consumption. By undertaking such a study,

Hughey made sociological insights and connections that would have been unavailable otherwise. For example, film critics are commonly thought of as providing judgment "as a result of their individual expertise, particular interests, or wisdom gained over their career." Hughey argues that this "is a sociologically uninformed view of film critics, as it portrays them as solitary beings relatively disconnected from one another and social currents in which they live." His findings showed, instead, that "critics interpret films within a specific community that structures a particular understanding and appraisal. Given that reviewers operate as mediating voices between the film's production and its consumption, their interpretations must find expression between the rock of the accurate product appraisal and the hard place of people's commonsense racial interpretations."

Hughey's mixed methods study thus constitutes three studies, with each pointing to a different aspect of culture. Weaving together these three approaches reveals how we, as a society, create and understand films and how films reflect contemporary political and cultural contexts.

part 4: innovations

The hallmark of methodological innovation is an improvement made to traditional methods by expanding the rate or cost of data collection, accessing hard-to-reach populations, or striving toward better generalizability and validity. Innovation, at its best, results in new types of data or new ways to collect data, new spaces for access, and even new forms of analysis. In some cases innovations are driven by new technologies, while in others they result from creative modifications and new applications of preexisting approaches. Innovation, in other words, can come in many forms. In this section, we offer four cases in which researchers built on traditional methodologies by incorporating a fresh methodological tool and one example of the creative application of preexisting tools.

As is so often the case, none of this comes easily. To be on the cutting edge of methodologies is thrilling: researchers get to experiment with novel approaches to traditional questions, play with previously unused technologies, and break new ground for future studies. Yet, being the first to implement a new technology can be daunting. There is little previous research to guide this work, nor is there always adequate infrastructural support. Most importantly, a good researcher should not employ a new methodology just *because* it's new. The new approach should be driven by the search for new or better answers. In addition, the researcher should not forget that the same guiding principles for good research apply even in the most novel settings.

As researchers push the field forward, they must avoid trying to reinvent the wheel. Each chapter describes the benefits of a particular innovation, but also reflects on its limits. These cases celebrate the risk-taking scholars who are making use of new technologies and approaches while also asking honest questions about whether an innovation can overcome the limitations of the traditional methods it is built on.

Daniel Sui talks us through the ethics of "big data," a pressing question in a world of data collection overdrive. This abundance of information offers exciting opportunities as well as important questions about ownership and access. **Justin Pickett** uses online surveys to quickly reach large pools of respondents at a fraction of the cost of previous studies. Similarly, **Francesca Polletta** capitalizes on an extensive Internet discussion forum to understand the role of storytelling in political views, while **Naomi Sugie** puts data collection into the hands of her respondents by developing smartphone apps to track their behavior, communication, and job search efforts after they leave prison. **Clifton Evers** looks to new video technology and straps a GoPro camera to his head and surfboard to conduct ethnographies of Australian surf communities. Finally, **Shamus Khan** presents us with a different type of innovation, incorporating spatial techniques traditionally used in studies of neighborhoods alongside historical and census data to understand the organization of social class in the orchestra hall.

finding findings in big data

FEATURING DANIEL SUI

14

Big data is making big buzz in the social sciences and beyond. Big data analyses take advantage of digital and statistical advances that provide more information about more people than has ever been available. The world of big data spans disciplines like marketing, social science, and health. In Sui's terms, "The applications of big data are limited only by your imagination," attracting the attention of industry, government, and academia.

Daniel Sui is an expert in such big data. In his view, big data is generally defined by the "three Vs": volume, variety, and velocity. The volume of data available today has sprung up because of the "growing, ubiquitous computing environment" that characterizes current society. "It doesn't matter where you look, whether the car you are driving, the cookware you're using in your kitchen, or the cell phone you use—everywhere you look, we are interacting with computers.

Every move we make in our daily lives will leave some footprint in cyberspace. That's the data that we leave in the cloud." Big data, then, is the information trail each one of us creates in our daily routines.

Data are coming fast and furious. As Sui explains, in the last three to five years, we've created more data than over the rest of human history combined. It's not only more data, but a greater variety of data, which means more options for analysis, including but not limited to quantitative statistical analysis, spatial mapping, data visualization, even textual or content analysis. Big data bridges the qualitative and quantitative divide and incorporates a wide variety of methodological approaches. "That's part of the beauty of big data. 'Data' traditionally means quantitative data. But in the age of big data, that means numbers, photographs, texts, all the blogs people have written, textual information, videos—everything that could be eventually translated into digital form. It's all part of the big data screen that you can use for further analysis."

For example, sociologists have long studied a phenomenon called "the strength of weak ties." This highly influential theory, developed by Mark Granovetter, argues that the majority of social structure and the transmission of most information comes through networks of weak social ties. However, as Sui describes, "for a long time we could only test the theory using a limited sample of social network data collected through surveys and interviews. Now, with big data approaches, computer scientists can collect millions of social media data points and can help sociologists test a long-discussed theory on a much more massive scale and detailed scale."

These types of interdisciplinary collaborations are important for harnessing the power of the data. "These days you need not only a quantitative analysis, but also a qualitative analysis. You need to connect the dots based on the variety of data you have. This is why storytelling is becoming more popular again as a methodological approach to deal with the big data screen." This helps explain the rising popularity and importance of developing a narrative to make better sense of the patterns in data.

ethical implications of big data

A unique limitation of big data relates to who owns or possesses it. In recent years, data ownership has been marked by a shift from academia and government to private corporations. This shift has created barriers to research. Further, even if the academic researchers have access, they may lack the technological infrastructure and resources to safely store or meaningfully analyze such large data sets. Sui argues that this shows a major shift in terms of "political power in the data—in the U.S., government agencies traditionally had custody of citizen data. But, these days, the power is shifting to the private sector. It's a few IT companies like Google, Apple, or Facebook who have collected a lot more data than the government has." Sui continues, "That's a significant game changer for all data-related analysis and applications."

Beyond ownership, how might big data change society? Sui cautions that these questions are new and important, yet unanswered: "That's another interdisciplinary approach we need to take for big data applications. It's no longer simply to get the data, do the analysis and to do the technical part. It's also to critically examine the social, political, legal, ethical implication." More broadly, Sui suggests this speaks to the need for social scientists to remain actively involved in the conversation. "In the big data age, I think that's probably the most important contribution a social scientist can make."

Big data analysis sometimes takes for granted that, because the samples are massive, they are also representative. Sui reminds us, however, that "we have to bear in mind that big data is, in a broader scheme of things, based on a biased population or a biased sample to begin with. It's very dangerous if we only draw a conclusion based on big data or develop policies exclusively based upon the availability of big data."

This is a result of what's called the digital divide. "It doesn't matter if we are talking about developed countries like North America or Western Europe or developing countries like in Latin America or parts of sub-Saharan Africa. There are still people not wired into this high-tech computing environment. They don't have a broadband Internet connection, they don't have a cell phone." So even big data is limited, and scholars must take care not to overgeneralize findings. "Yes, big data is useful," Sui says. "But it only reveals patterns or addresses issues for those people who are actually part of the computing environment. It is a duty for social scientists to keep that in mind when they work with big data, so that we can find creative ways to get to these folks and see that whatever they are experiencing is reflected in our research, and that their issues and concerns get addressed adequately."

Sharpening our research questions and focusing on stronger interdisciplinary collaboration will likely help academics wade into and sort through the wealth of data. "Many of the issues or the challenging questions we are trying to address, no single discipline can adequately handle those research questions. It requires social scientists, natural scientists, computer engineers, and folks from humanities working together to connect the dots." By coming together, researchers can synthesize vast amounts of information, develop coherent narratives, and shed new light on questions of social equity, environmental sustainability, and a host of other creative questions.

we are all big data

A major benefit of big data is that it's everywhere, all the time! This means new opportunities for those first becoming exposed to social research. For instance, students can begin by simply studying the behavior of their circle of friends on social media or by developing their own web-crawling programs to collect data themselves. Most importantly, playing with big data will help students and researchers "sharpen their technical skills to analyze those data and integrate both quantitative and qualitative approaches to develop coherent analysis and synthesis of the data they collected."

In this way, big data is actually more approachable than many might guess. By using it to help ask and answer basic social questions with tried-and-true analytic techniques, we can fulfill the promise of the massive data sets to which we all contribute. As Sui puts it, "Both you and me are big data creators. Seventy percent of big data are created by users through their daily activities, so why not just take advantage of using the data that we create ourselves?"

online surveys

FEATURING JUSTIN PICKETT

S urveys are a time-tested tool used to gather information on people's activities and beliefs and to assess public opinion. While "random digit dialing" to landline
telephones has long been favored, fielding surveys on the
Internet is gaining popularity. Justin Pickett walks us through
the logic of survey research and discusses Internet surveys
as a new take on this traditional method. This new approach
is both convenient and cost-effective: going online signals a
shift from accessing subjects through phone, mail, or in person to surveying subjects at their own time of convenience.

The cost is also incredibly low compared to phone or in-
person survey methods, making this approach increasingly
attractive to budget-minded researchers. For instance, surveys that rely on a probability sample (a pool of respondents
statistically representative of the U.S. population as a whole)
are often managed by large companies. A company recruits
these large pools of potential respondents and calls on them

to answer surveys periodically. Pickett's last survey using a company like this cost $90,000.

Less traditional approaches turn this model upside down. Survey Monkey, for instance, has an "audience panel"—a group of 400,000 respondents who go online and take surveys at a time that is convenient for them. Because the pool is so large, it provides solid coverage of the geographic and demographic contours of the United States. The same survey that cost $90,000, cost $5,000 conducted through this method. A third option for online surveys is to use a crowdsourcing Web site like Amazon's Mechanical Turk. In this scenario, respondents sign up as "workers" and can search surveys and tasks for which they will be paid a small sum. This approach cost Pickett $200. Thus, the Internet widens the net and levels the playing field for who gets to conduct—and respond to—social science surveys.

challenges

Pickett reports a "ton of challenges" associated with moving surveys online. "The thing is, online surveys are amazing and while they have a lot of good strengths, they also have a lot of ways that you can mess up if you're not careful."

One limitation is their visual nature: "Everything matters, from the color of the screen to everything *on* the screen." The pictures, layout, and font might serve as unintended prompts, priming people to answer a certain way. For instance, one study found that if respondents selected responses from a list of words, they were more likely to rank items at the top of the list as "better." This is called the "top-is-good" heuristic.

A different experiment showed one group of respondents a picture of someone shopping in a grocery store, while another group got a picture of someone shopping for clothes. The survey then asked the respondent how many times they'd been shopping in the last month. "The people who got the picture of the person shopping in a clothes store estimated significantly fewer times than the people who got the picture of the person in the grocery store. This is because the grocery store 'primed' them by giving a frequent exemplar, something you do commonly, whereas you don't shop as often for clothes. It's little things like that." Another example Pickett cites is of a survey where respondents were asked to describe their own health. Respondents who saw a photo of a woman jogging were more likely to describe their health as poor, compared to a group who saw a photo of a woman in a hospital. Pickett explains that respondents were likely comparing their health to the image they saw. Pickett calls this a "contrast effect—it just shows how anything you have on the screen, if you're not careful, can prime people."

Using online surveys also complicates more traditional sampling strategies. To combat this, researchers should think about strategies to deal with three potential issues: (1) respondents using false identities; (2) respondents who complete the same survey more than once; and (3) respondents who rush through the survey without providing honest and thoughtful responses. Another important issue is how the online format might change the way a research subject understands a question. For instance, Pickett explains how researchers might bias their results for a study on presidential approval by asking respondents questions about their family economic situations immediately before asking them how they think the president is doing. Because it is easy to edit online surveys, however, a researcher could easily shift the order of questions or test out multiple versions of the survey to check for question-order effects. This is one of the many benefits of the newly emerging field of web surveys.

A final key issue is that it's impossible to reach everybody using web surveys; not everyone has access to the Internet. Echoing Daniel Sui's comments in Chapter 14, Pickett reports that only around 78% of adults in the United States have access to the Internet. Even if they were all included in a potential sample, coverage bias would *still* be a problem. Specifically, people who use the Internet tend to be younger, better educated, have higher incomes, and tend to be white rather than black or Hispanic. All this makes it difficult to obtain a representative sample.

benefits

The cost-effectiveness of online surveys is quite appealing. As Pickett describes it, "I think that you never want to say that money is a big thing, but I think cost really is." He cautions that "good science is not fast and it's not cheap. But, if you go out and you spend $200,000 on a survey with bad measures and bad theoretical hypotheses, you're wasting money and time." A good strategy, according to Pickett, is to use the less expensive online option to pilot test a survey before applying for a large grant to replicate the survey using more traditional methods and at a nationally representative scale.

Because not all researchers have large pools of funding, the method thus offers an excellent entry point: "A lot of people have great, great ideas. They just don't have the resources to go out and do a longitudinal study of youths in the city, for example. So I think giving people the tools to initially test their idea and get it out there benefits science, as long as you're aware of the limitations. It opens the theorizing and research to a broader set of people."

Online surveys are new terrain, but Pickett argues that we should be open to new methods:

Sometimes the newness of something scares people. It may very well be that, ten years from now, we find out that web surveys were horrible and that ten years' worth of research really was counterproductive. It may happen. But, web surveys can help us access people of all ages and educations, who live all across the United States. We need to work on the ability to not get scared because of the newness, and to focus on the fact that we can relatively cheaply get data that is externally quite valid. I think it's of real benefit. I hope more people do it, even though there's risk!

online forums and deliberative storytelling

FEATURING FRANCESCA POLLETTA

16

P olitical researchers have long claimed that discourse and conversation are good for democracy. Now that political conversations are increasingly happening online, researchers like Francesca Polletta have new opportunities to directly access and analyze the way people discuss politics or "how people talk in public about issues they care about." In particular, Polletta seeks to understand "how people imagine their political worlds operating. How do they see themselves acting in their political worlds? What limits do they see to their ability to effect change? How are their political imaginations limited or bounded?"

Here, Polletta walks us through an innovative project that brings together qualitative and quantitative approaches to better understand the role of storytelling in political discourse. In this project, she treats the online setting as "natural" since the researcher is completely absent from the exchanges taking place. To her, the data she can glean from

Internet conversations offer a different kind of authenticity than surveys, interviews, or even in-person ethnographies.

the forum

Polletta's study focused on public deliberation about how to rebuild the World Trade Center site in the wake of 9/11. "In the last 15 years or so, scholars of democracy have argued powerfully that political talk is very important to the vitality of polities. There's been a great emphasis on encouraging people to talk in public about issues they care about." However, Polletta explains, "We have plenty of examples of political talk that is not successful (think, for example, of the town hall meetings about health-care reform in 2009, where political talk was extreme, inflammatory, and led people to disagree more than they otherwise would)." Political scholars have argued that, in fact, *deliberative* talk and open debate should be encouraged. "The hope is that if people are encouraged to engage in this kind of deliberation, it will have all kinds of positive political effects. It will lead to citizens becoming more informed, it will lead them to trust their political institutions, as well as leading to better policies." Polletta sought to provide us a better understanding of what this talk actually looks like and does.

The online forum under study was actually a follow-up to a 4,500-person event held in a convention center in lower Manhattan. The audience gathered to deliberate about what to build at the site of the former World Trade Center. The public event was followed by a two-week online discussion in the summer of 2002: "The online forum offered us a fantastic opportunity to look at how different groups talk about the same things. Because there were over 800 people who participated, they were assigned to 25 different groups that all followed the same agenda. This feature of the online forum made it a wonderful opportunity to actually compare how people talk."

The data came in the form of thousands of posts. Online participants began by introducing themselves to the group, then talked about their aspirations for what should be built in lower Manhattan. The options brought in a range of civic topics, including economic development issues, transportation issues, parks and recreation, and, of course, the choice of an appropriate memorial for Ground Zero.

Polletta was particularly interested in the role that stories played in the forum. Respondents often shared personal experiences and testimony instead of logic or reasons. "We had an opportunity to see just how people use stories and reasons in actual deliberation. We could see if people were marginalized if they used storytelling to get their points across instead of abstract, logical discourse."

dealing with data

Polletta and John Lee examined qualities of these online group discussions, such as the length of messages and how many people participated. To dig into the storytelling aspect of group discussion, the research team focused on 12 groups, reading through all the online posts and coding them. They focused on how people made arguments: whether they used stories or abstract reasons, who used each, and how they responded to one another: "We were interested not only in when people turned to using a story rather than a reason, but also, whether telling a story worked. Are people persuaded by stories?"

The project made use of qualitative and quantitative analysis. Polletta used logistic regression to measure the likelihood that someone would tell a story or give a reason. Then, her team went deeper with an interpretive qualitative analysis of the general patterns identified in the quantitative data. When combined, the process went something like this: The quantitative analysis showed that people tended to tell stories when they saw themselves as having an unpopular point of view. Digging into the specific conversations, Polletta then saw instances where forum participants might say something like, "'Most people believe that the towers should be rebuilt, but I don't.' Then they would tell a story." In this way, the qualitative analysis helped illuminate and explain the storytelling patterns across groups.

Issues of validity are especially challenging when researchers aim to discover meaning. Polletta argues that "the virtue of this kind of coding-of-talk is that you can get at people's beliefs as they articulate them. So it's very different from an interview, or a setting where someone is really trying to put their best foot forward. Here you see them talking about the issues that concern them in a natural setting."

Generalizability was also a concern, since the public deliberation that followed 9/11 "was, in many ways, unlike any other public deliberation. This was following up on a tragedy of massive proportions." That said, Polletta argues, "In fact, many public deliberative forums are about emotional issues, such as cancer or police brutality. But, more importantly, in the public deliberative forum that we studied, the vast majority of people's comments were not about their own experience of 9/11. They really were telling much more prosaic stories about things like which restaurants they liked to go to or what was important to them in the way their downtown was organized."

Because this is an innovative approach, scholars have only just begun to explore the generalizability of data from Internet forums. As Polletta describes it, "I think our final answer to the question of generalizability is that this is one study of one public deliberative forum and to understand better how public deliberation operates, we need more studies of other forums."

lessons learned

Polletta's innovative, blended approach has advantages for a deep understanding of the data: While the quantitative approach identified patterns across many individuals, the qualitative analysis provided insight into the processes behind these patterns. The online context, in turn, provided a neutral environment for people to openly discuss their views and tell stories—all in a documented space.

One example from the study shows the development of Polletta's understanding of the online forum:

> One of the things we found was that people would often say something like, "I agree completely with what you just said" after someone told a story, and then they would tell their own story. We know that's quite common—that when someone tells a story, often times a member of the audience will respond with their own story. But what was interesting to us was that people often followed up with a story that made a completely different point. For example, one person told a story about how upsetting it was that tourists were descending on Ground Zero. She felt that it was disrespectful to the tragedy that had

taken place there. And another participant responded, "I agree with you completely," and then told her own story, which was not critical of the people descending upon Ground Zero. Instead, she said, "They're pilgrims, they need to understand what happened." Then, a third participant weighed in and brought the two views together by saying, "People can't really understand what happened, but they try as best they can, and how terrible it is that people criticize them."

In this sense, stories offered a way for people to disagree without antagonizing each other or appearing hostile. Polletta explains, "One of the things that we know from studies of public deliberation is that people are really worried that other people will disagree with them. They see it as an attack on them. What these exchanges suggested to us is that telling a story may be a way to disagree with someone without seeming to disagree."

The online environment is an important and rapidly growing space for social and political research, particularly for those interested in deliberative exchanges. As Polletta reminds us, "We've long known that conversations give us powerful access to the meanings that shape behavior, but the question is: what chunk of conversation do we study?" The online forums provided a "glimpse of how people think about their worlds, not when asked by a survey researcher, but when they're talking with other people who either share their political views, or may have different views." These are powerful sites for considering how the makeup of a group shapes conversation, storytelling, and successful arguments. Put simply, "it gives us access to people's political beliefs in a natural setting."

understanding behavior through smartphones

FEATURING NAOMI SUGIE

I n her study of people searching for jobs after being released from prison, Naomi Sugie realized she could use smartphones as an exciting data collection tool for real-time data.

Indeed, researchers have begun to create software applications for phones that can passively collect all kinds of information. Things like location, call logs, text messaging, and the use of social media apps are all collected without interrupting the research participants' daily lives. Researchers can also actively collect data from smartphones by sending automated surveys to participants during the day. These surveys might measure experiences, attitudes, and emotions as things are actually happening.

apps for reentry

Sugie's research is part of a bigger study called the Newark Smartphone Reentry Project. The primary aim of the project is to understand the on-the-ground experiences of an individual leaving prison, reentering the community, and searching for employment. The immediate months after prison are a challenging and critical time, as individuals reintegrate into society, reestablish relationships, and face the barriers their criminal conviction builds in finding housing and employment. However, existing research on reentry had key limitations. According to Sugie, "Previous reentry research used periodic interviews to ask retrospective questions about what occurred since the last interview, but these studies often had relatively high rates of attrition over the study period because of the challenges of reentry. We thought that smartphones might be a way to more effectively follow individuals with unstable living situations and contact information. Smartphones would more accurately measure their experiences."

Because Sugie was utilizing a new methodology, she collaborated with software developers to create a smartphone application that could passively collect behavioral information, such as users' geographic locations as well as limited call and text log information. She also added a functionality to "push" surveys to individuals at automated times.

Her team partnered with the Newark parole office to recruit participants for the study. Because smartphones are a new data collection tool, 80% of the participants were randomly assigned to the group using smartphones for data collection, while the other 20% were assessed using more traditional methods, like brief check-in interviews each week. For the researchers, setting up a control and a treatment group provided a way to check that the data they were collecting with the smartphones were similar to the patterns observed in the other group.

Pushing out surveys to participants via their smartphones was particularly innovative. The research participants would hear a notification bell when one of three types of quick survey was ready for them: There was an "experience sampling survey," which was a very brief survey at a random time each day to sample participants' day-to-day experiences; a "retrospective survey," which came at 7:00 p.m. every day and asked respondents about their job-seeking activities that day; and a 10- to 15-second survey that came automatically after the participant received a call or a text from a new phone number. This survey asked a few basic questions about the person who had just contacted the phone's owner and allowed researchers to capture, in particular, job leads.

the findings

The study yielded two important findings. First, previous research, Sugie explains, "typically considers everyone to be in the same or similar boat when they come out of prison, and there's not a lot of focus on the heterogeneity that exists, particularly in terms of their employment prospects." Sugie suspects this is actually due to the lack of detailed information about individuals going through reentry. Using smartphones, Sugie found three distinct day-to-day patterns among the participants, naming the groups "searchers, nonsearchers, and workers" to denote how actively they searched for work (either they drop out of the labor market after a couple weeks, search for employment the whole time, or ultimately find a job). These distinctions are important for tailoring pre- and postrelease programming and social services for those undergoing reentry. Sugie says, "We might imagine that individuals in each of these different subgroups or typologies would benefit from very different types of reentry employment services that are catered to their specific needs."

Another dominant theme in existing research was that reentering individuals are socially isolated with fragmented social networks. Sugie's data dispute this claim: "Despite participants' comments to me that they generally keep to themselves, I found most were highly connected socially and communicated with lots of individuals. I've examined a variety of different data sources, like interviews, smartphone surveys, call logs, and behavioral measures, and they all suggest that reentering individuals are much more socially connected than previous scholarship had assumed."

the tricks of new tech

Smartphones yield information that helps answer theoretically rich but hard-to-measure research questions. For example, Sugie notes that much research focuses on the spatial mismatch between jobs and people in urban areas, which contributes to high levels of unemployment among the lowest-skilled urban residents:

"While we know that there have been these major economic changes and movements of jobs to suburban areas over the past few decades, there's not been a lot of research on how these cultural trends really translate at the level of individuals and impact their day-to-day job search," Sugie told us. "Instead of using measures of reported residential addresses, we could use real-time information on the geographic regions where participants spent their time. This helps us understand how spatial mismatch really affects people trying to find work."

She also offered some cautions. First, sociologists are rarely trained as software engineers. For this reason, it is important to have good computer science collaborators and to have good cross-disciplinary conversations. Because smartphones are new and relatively untested data collection tools, there are not yet established best practices for data collection, storage, and security, and it is imperative that social scientists discuss the nitty-gritty technical aspects of their design with people familiar with the most up-to-date approaches.

Sugie also cautions against thinking smartphones are a silver bullet for researchers. In many ways, they are only suited—for now—for collecting certain types of self-report information. Surveys designed for smartphones are best when asking multiple-choice or very short questions, making them perhaps too restrictive for studies where nuanced or complex answers are required.

Researchers are only beginning to understand how best to interpret and analyze the data. Even Sugie is still grappling with how accurately the information her team collected reflects the participants' lives. "Phones are not people, and the data is only really reliable if participants are using the phones as the researcher assumes. We're still trying to assess what potential biases could be related to smartphone-based data and whether those biases are different for certain groups of people as opposed to other groups."

benefits and possibilities

Because interview methods, retrospective self-reports, and administrative records searches are such long-standing data sources, researchers often overlook their limitations. Sugie's use of smartphones opens the door to measuring and documenting "the actual realities of participants that are simply not possible to assess using traditional measures." Smartphones can also provide an enormous amount of data, lending a rich and descriptive documentation of a period in an individual's life. Sugie believes more work using data collection apps and pop-up phone surveys could greatly expand knowledge on social behavior, and she invites researchers to consider questions and ideas we were not able to measure before. With those questions, she encourages developing data collection software applications with potential outside the academy. For instance, Sugie was acutely interested in contributing knowledge that would be useful for reentry programs, so along with the functions she needed in her data collection app, Sugie also helped develop a peer-based group text-messaging forum within the app. Program participants could communicate through the app with others in similar situations. For Sugie, "That's an example of an intervention that is free for practitioners and can be easily adopted into programming."

wearable technology
and visual analysis

FEATURING CLIFTON EVERS

18

W hile technological innovation is more often associated with new ways of gathering or processing quantitative data, employers of qualitative methods can also benefit. Clifton Evers's work on surfing and masculinity provides illustration.

Evers builds on the classic approach to ethnography through use of a GoPro video camera. Field-based video ethnography has a long history (particularly within anthropology), but taking footage on the move has not been easy. Technological development has provided researchers with cameras that can be brought into a variety of new places, attached to new equipment, and used to gather previously unattainable data. In this chapter, we join Evers out in the waves to understand how using a mobile recording device helped document previously unrecognized elements of masculinity among surfers. We then follow Evers back to shore as he takes further advantage of the new technology by widely sharing his footage with other researchers, surfers, and the general public.

capturing emotion and affect

Like C. J. Pascoe's journey into high school hallways, Evers's research was motivated by the sense that something was missing in classic studies of masculinity that depicted men as simply stoic, unemotional, and strong. "I knew this just wasn't how my mates were. They liked to put on that front, but when you went surfing with them or participated in sport with them, it was a very emotional, affective experience, and they'd express this in particular ways. And this would lead into other conversations, be it about relationships, their health, their family life, or their relationships with each other."

Evers wanted to know, "What roles do emotions and affects play in the lives of men, and how do they make sense of those lives?" Evers, a relatively inexperienced researcher at the time, initially turned to interviews and focus groups—"Of course this was an abject failure, because they're just not going to talk about what their bodies are going through, what their emotional state was at a particular point in time, these were not conversations that they were willing to have, especially with the other guys present."

Evers also had to find the theories that could help him understand what he was seeing and provide the language to formulate effective questions. "Every time I started trying to articulate what my body was experiencing, the sensations: words weren't quite capturing it, and it was then that I had to dig into the affect literature." Affect is what is felt at the level of the body, and it can be understood as pre- or nonconscious sensations. In contrast, emotions are what happen when we try to make *sense* of the affective experience. Or, as Evers explains, "Emotions are when culture and the social come rushing in to explain the immediacy of what we're experiencing."

As an avid surfer, Evers had an easy entry into his fieldwork site: the "lineup" out in the waves at popular and hidden Australian surf spots. Rather than relying on just memory and field notes taken after he dried off, Evers decided he should use video to capture the embodied experience. His inspiration came from the art world:

Tracy Moffatt is an indigenous artist from Australia. Her film *Heaven,* about Australian surfers, basically flipped the gauge. She took a hand-held camera and starts the footage shooting them changing on the street into and out of their wetsuits. She starts from a long way away and slowly interferes and gets closer, and closer, and closer, until she's tearing the towels off of them. This is all done without planning, but she totally gets involved. It just alters the whole dynamic. And conversations would emerge: the camera was playing its role, she was playing with the power dynamics, and there was this sort of creative process, and I said, "Well, why can't I use a similar process?"

At first, Evers's options were limited. He was a poor student. Cameras were expensive and land-bound—a problem, since the men's performances of masculinity were more controlled when they were on land, rather than bobbing on their boards in the surf. "What a lot of the men would speak about, or what they experienced in terms of emotions, affect, and embodied experience was happening in the water. So how does one do video research in the sea?" Then along came the GoPro—a small, robust, waterproof, and relatively cheap video camera: "I could attach it to a surfboard, I could carry it in my mouth, and I could strap it around my neck. It allowed me to surf and keep my hands free." Evers was also able to hold the camera in his hand and scan the lineup to get a fuller picture of the social and embodied dynamics.

the reveal

The video footage made clear that, despite the men's difficulty in discussing emotion and their relationships with each other and their claims to having good control over those emotions, well, they were wrong. The men became emotional and the affects of fear, joy, and anger leapt from body to body as they encountered the surf. Evers explains that, in the water, "nothing is ever settled." In one moment, the men's actions, even how they line up in the water, follow the traditional modes of masculinity, "but the very next moment, a particular wave appears and everything gets shaken up as people renegotiate the pecking order—people express anger, people get afraid— the whole dynamic is shifting and adapting all the time." The camera was able to pick up more detail than any ethnographer or surfer could. "For example, I've got hundreds and hundreds and hundreds of expressions and images of surfers' faces. This is affect working. There's no way they could have spoken about that—they didn't even know they were doing it half the time!"

The footage unexpectedly pushed Evers to take the mundane, peripheral, and often-ignored seriously. Whether it was a minor argument among a subsection of the group or surfers happily welcoming back a long-absent rider, the camera captured it all. "You see all the back-slapping and the handshakes and the smiles spreading throughout the lineup, and then somebody would cry out, 'Hey, welcome back!' sort of thing, and then he'd paddle over and they'd give each other a hug." While these events would likely not make it to an ethnographer's notepad, "the camera, because it uses a fish-eye lens, which gathers quite a wide area, would pick up on things. I'd be watching the footage back and I'd go, 'Ah, look what was going on over there.' I was focusing on the wave coming at me, trying to avoid it, and completely ignoring that emotional and affective bonding."

These "aha" moments moved Evers beyond his focus on major moments of intensity, which already get so much play in masculinity studies. Increasingly, he began paying attention to all the *other* moments: "The vast majority of time, affect is muted. . . . These major events or these events that stand out to us are not the only things going on." It is here, during the overlooked moments of downtime, that much of the connection between the men occurs.

access

Access is a central challenge in any qualitative work, ethnography particularly. In this case, Evers had surfed since he was a young boy. "I was a local at a particular spot and that gave me unprecedented access to a very close-knit group of men. But when I expanded the research to other areas (other surfing locations and local groups of surfers), I had to go through gatekeepers. Fortunately, I knew people who could do that." Without his initial start at a familiar site, his unique form of snowball sampling would have been difficult—"If you've never surfed before, how do you go out and gather surfing footage? In the locations that I was going to, it's almost impossible."

Insider status does bring some difficulties. Researchers may feel a sense of obligation to the group under study: "Sometimes I found myself caught up in a process of saying, 'If I share this footage, what does that do to my own sense of belonging, my future access to these groups?'" Evers continues, "Sometimes what's revealed isn't pretty, and the results of your research can be difficult for the people who you're doing research with. But it can equally be difficult for you, because you will end up outside." Even though Evers always clearly explained what he was researching, the footage could capture aspects of surfing culture that its participants did not want to see: "You'd gather this footage, and an ugly side would come out, like, people think surfing is all fun and play, but it gets 'aggro.' Or people show their fear or they would demonstrate just how they are on the periphery—they like to think that they belong, but then when you watch back the footage, you see that the others in the group keep them at a distance. They don't like to watch that back." In other cases, the presence of the camera was seen as a threat to surfers who were protective of particularly coveted and often secret surf spots. In extreme cases, this even led to violence, "with my cameras being smashed … or taken from me and never returned, despite my pleading."

sharing the field

Video ethnography provides compelling stories and data, but much is lost in the translation from rich life world to written word. This is particularly challenging when attempting to describe footage that captures as embodied and sensuous a practice as surfing. "Academic writing is notoriously boring. How does one communicate affect and emotion?"

For Evers, making the video footage available is an important way of not only sharing the experience but also encouraging greater intellectual engagement. Specifically, Evers chooses to share the complete footage rather than editing it down to convey a particular argument. It's not that he doesn't know how to edit video (although Evers was quick to note, "I'm not a filmmaker!"). Instead, he sees the footage as data that should remain unaltered: "People edit out a lot of ethnographic footage and they piece together a particular narrative, present a particular representation. And that's well and good, but when you see footage, I always go, 'What happened in between here and here?' All the dull, mundane, boring stuff is taken out (and this particularly happens with surfing and sports stuff) and I want all that left in—the bobbing up and down for an hour and the sheer look of boredom on some of the participants' faces, I want it all. So I'm going to release a two-hour session, no editing whatsoever, so other researchers or other people can watch this and unpack it from their own particular subjective positions."

Evers sees his data sharing as an essential step in promoting interdisciplinary conversation, too: "There's no mystery here; let's just lay the cards on the table." He continues, "I don't want to tell you what is, I want to see what could happen with this. What can we do with it? What can *we* do with it?"

When asked why someone might consider adopting his method, Evers's answer is refreshingly candid: "It's a hell of a lot of fun. I love it. I absolutely love it." Not only does he get to spend his days in the ocean, the camera has revealed previously ignored interactions. And the camera can even draw people in—"people will see the camera, they'll come talk to me, say, 'What are you doing?' We'll have a chat, and then it opens up a whole dialogue, so that's been a real buzz that comes out of it."

historical data and the spatial analysis of class

FEATURING SHAMUS KHAN

19

S hamus Khan offers a compelling example of how methodological innovation does not necessarily require a new technology or analytic tool. Instead, innovation can emerge from creative tweaks to tried-and-true methods or from combining approaches culled from within and outside the discipline. To close this volume, Khan discusses his research on the subscribers to the New York Philharmonic from 1842 to the present day. His work offers us a way to better understand working with large historical data sets and the incorporation of spatial analytic techniques to understand the creation and reproduction of class.

Khan's project takes on the rather straightforward task of looking at who has attended the New York Philharmonic over the last 150 years. The project builds on his interest in the relationship between culture and the formation of class. "We think about culture as a kind of resource, but we don't have a whole lot of historical information about cultural participation and what people were actually doing." The massive data set allowed Khan to ask a series of key questions related to class formation, including, what is the role of an elite social form like classical music? What role did the orchestra play in defining and constituting a class of elite New Yorkers over a long period of time, and how does that change? And, conversely, how did the elite New Yorkers change their relationship with classed practices like the orchestra over time?

falling into data

One of the most unique qualities of Khan's project is the data. As Khan explains, "I was basically given a data set to generate a question." The New York Philharmonic had just received $10 million to digitize its entire archive. However, before beginning this rather massive undertaking, they needed to demonstrate that it would be of interest to people who weren't musicologists. They were aware of Khan due to his background as a musician, and approached him to see if there were any potential social science studies hidden within the data. "And, as somebody who was interested in elites, I began to puzzle through: Well, what *could* we know here?" Khan continues, "In other bits of my work I've talked about the ways in which we often rely upon self-reports and what people say, and this was something very different. It was giving me actual practice, so I didn't have to look back and see what people say about classical music and whether or not they liked it. I could look at butts in seats and see who was actually sitting in the hall."

Moving forward, Khan's methodological design was built around gathering three very simple pieces of information: the name and physical address of a subscriber and the location of their philharmonic concert seats. "If you imagine the concert hall as a kind of physical space with a bunch of seat locations, I know where you're located. This allowed us to look at residential dynamics mapped onto cultural dynamics." Khan was making use of traditional methodological approaches to generate new types of connections and questions. "A lot of work in sociology looks at the dynamics of neighborhoods and how the dynamics of neighborhoods change. I could look at that, because I knew where people lived over time in this data set, but then I could also look at where they 'lived' in a concert hall; that is, the places that they chose to sit. So the question became: Could I think about the relationship between residential dynamics and cultural dynamics by constructing an account of 'place' or where people were placed or located, both in the city and in this physical hall?"

As Khan and his research assistants traveled down this path, it quickly became clear that they needed *more* data. They did not want to assume people in the hall were elites, and instead sought secondary information to confirm their socio-economic status. This allowed them to compare the people in the orchestra hall to other kinds of elites. "The first thing that we did was look to see if any of these people were listed in the social register. The social register is a registry of prominent people in the city of New York, it makes up 0.1% of the city overall, but it used to be referred to as the 'Stud Book.' The Stud Book was where you would go to find an eligible man for a daughter of yours to marry."

This information allowed Khan to see where people fit into the broader social ecology, as well as how they compared to other members of the social elite. Finally, Khan used the census records to learn the occupations of all the concert attendees: "This gave us a lot of information about where people lived, what social clubs they were a part of, how they compared to other people who were in similar social clubs, and their professions. This was the big data that we were able to analyze."

established techniques, new applications

There is a trend within quantitative work to celebrate the fanciest, shiniest new method of analysis. However, Khan is quick to remind researchers not to forget the classics. "The first thing you should do when looking at something like this is just look at a distribution or look at the simplest descriptive statistics. They help you understand your data, and they are often pretty accurate." Khan combined these basic descriptives with spatial autocorrelation—a form of analysis commonly employed by geographers and users of GIS.

"This was basically imagining I picked somebody in the hall and asked them to look at the 25 people closest to them. What is the likelihood that those 25 people are also their closest neighbors outside of the hall?" If elites were consolidating, the spatial autocorrelation should reflect that. In other words, "the predictive capacity of your 25 closest neighbors in the hall should be greater over time as people move closer together in the hall and closer together in the city."

Through use of a methodological technique not as common in sociology or in historical studies, Khan was able to confirm his suspicion.

Then what it requires is taking one step back and asking: What's driving that phenomenon? What we're able to show is that the people in the balcony seats are increasingly likely to come from different neighborhoods than the people in the box seats (the box seats are the good seats, the balcony seats are the bad seats). And so the autocorrelations are driven basically by rich people clustering and poorer people clustering (though they're not poor, they're middle class) closer together both in the hall and in the city. But the reason the rich people are clustering closer and closer together is because there's a new group that's different from them, people who I basically identify as high-cultural-capital Jews who are driving the economically rich people closer to one another. So the process of consolidation of the elite is in part an *inclusionary* one. Because as this new group gets included in this practice, they are partially driving this phenomenon of elite consolidation.

Khan's findings challenge the dominant understanding of class formation in New York in the late 19th century. "The idea of consolidation was that, over the course of the long Gilded Age—the period of the second big industrial revolution—what elites did is they became more consolidated; they became increasingly more alike. . . . If you look at things like how many pieces are played by the New York Philharmonic, that story's absolutely true, but if you look at the data we gathered, it actually turns out not to be true."

In the case of historical data, some information is simply lost to the sands of time. Khan provides an example: "For about 70% of the population, we were able to identify their profession. To be able to identify people's professions in the 1880s is pretty great. It was much higher than what I thought we'd be able to do. However, that 30% that we don't have, maybe those are people who are systematically missing, and so that's going to bias our results." The basic concern is that those who are represented in the available data are those who left a "bigger historical footprint"; the missing group is likely not random, but marginalized.

The other issue that Khan and his researchers faced was a 1921 fire that had destroyed the 1890 census data. That information is simply gone. "We have to assume that somebody's profession in 1880 or in 1900 reflects what their 1890 profession would be. It is not likely that people change radically their professions at this period in time, but still we have to make pretty huge assumptions."

providing shoulders to stand on

Khan's findings on the practices and movement of elites in New York City is a valuable contribution to our understanding of class formation, yet perhaps its greatest contribution will be its methodological innovation. As Khan demonstrates, the approach truly matters for understanding actual patterns. Had he utilized the same approach previous historians and sociologists chose, he would have replicated the same story. "To me, that shows that we're not actually studying a different kind of phenomenon; we're studying the same phenomenon differently."

Spatial analysis like the kind Khan's team performed is most commonly used in neighborhood-level studies, but it has enormous potential in other social spaces (like the orchestra hall). Khan tells us, "I'm now interested in the same phenomenon with church pews and basically what the role of elite religiosity is in the city of New York." This interest in extending a methodological innovation is the test of the value and generalizability of the method. "If I can deploy this same kind of technique in a different context and generate some results, I have a little bit of a firmer leg to stand on."

In a reflection that captures the essence of scientific progress, Khan understands that the goal is not to be right, but to be a little *more* right. "Chances are that the finding will be roughly correct for a period of time and then wrong. . . . What I would hope for over the next 20 years is that other people whittle away at the explanation, and they say, 'Well, it's an okay explanation, but actually we can do a little bit better.'"

about the authors

Kyle Green is an Assistant Professor of Sociology and Head of Gender Studies at Utica College. He received his PhD in sociology from the University of Minnesota in 2015 and his MA in geography in 2008. A qualitative scholar, Green researches physical practice, storytelling, intimacy, and the body. With Sarah Lageson, he is the founding co-producer of the Give Methods a Chance podcast and Office Hours podcast, and was a founding editorial board member of The Society Pages.

Sarah Lageson is an Assistant Professor at Rutgers University–Newark School of Criminal Justice. She received her PhD in sociology from the University of Minnesota in 2015. A mixed methods scholar, Lageson researches technology, criminal justice, law, and punishment. With Kyle Green, she is the founding co-producer of the Give Methods a Chance podcast and Office Hours podcast, and was a founding editorial board member of The Society Pages.

about the contributors

Andrew Billings is Ronald Reagan Endowed Chair in Broadcasting in the College of Communication and Information Sciences at the University of Alabama and the director of the Alabama Program in Sports Communication. He is the author of 11 books, including *Olympic Media: Inside the Biggest Show on Television* (2008, Routledge) and *The Fantasy Sport Industry: Games within Games* (2014, Routledge).

Deborah Carr is in the sociology department at Boston University. She is the author of *Worried Sick: How Stress Hurts Us and How to Bounce Back* (2014, Rutgers University Press) and the coauthor of *The Art and Science of Social Research* (W. W. Norton) and *Introduction to Sociology* (W. W. Norton), now in its Tenth Edition.

David Cook-Martín is in the sociology department at Grinnell College. He studies migration and citizenship policy and is the co-author, with David FitzGerald, of *Culling the*

Masses: The Democratic Origins of Racist Immigration Policies in the Americas (2014, Harvard University Press).

Clifton Evers is in the media and cultural studies department at Newcastle University. He studies gender, leisure, mobile media, action/lifestyle sports, and emotion.

David FitzGerald is Theodore E. Gildred Chair in U.S.–Mexican Relations at the University of California, San Diego. He is also the co-director of the Center for Comparative Immigration Studies. He is the co-author, with David Cook-Martín, of *Culling the Masses: The Democratic Origins of Racist Immigration Policies in the Americas* (2014, Harvard University Press).

Keith Hampton is in the department of media and information at Michigan State University. He studies community and the relationship between digital technologies, social networks, democratic engagement, and the urban environment.

Matthew Hughey is in the department of sociology at the University of Connecticut. He is the author of *White Bound: Nationalists, Antiracists, and the Shared Meanings of Race* (2012, Stanford University Press).

Shamus Khan is in the sociology department at Columbia University. He is the author of *Privilege: The Making of an Adolescent Elite at St. Paul's School* (2011, Princeton University Press) and the co-author of *The Practice of Research* (2013, Oxford University Press).

Audrey Kobayashi is in the department of geography and planning at Queen's University. She studies how the processes of human differentiation, including race, class, gender, and national ability, emerge in places such as the home, street, and workplace. She is the co-author of *The International Encyclopedia of Geography* (forthcoming, Wiley Blackwell) and *Remaking Human Geography* (2016, Routledge), now in its Second Edition.

Helen B. Marrow is in the sociology department at Tufts University. She studies immigration, race and ethnicity, social class, health, and inequality and social policy. She is the author of *New Destination Dreaming: Immigration, Race, and Legal Status in the Rural American South* (2011, Stanford University Press).

Devah Pager is in the sociology department at Harvard University. She is the author of *Marked: Race, Crime, and*

Finding Work in an Era of Mass Incarceration (University of Chicago, 2007).

C. J. Pascoe is in the sociology department at the University of Oregon. She studies masculinity, youth, homophobia, sexuality, and new media. She is the author of *Dude, You're a Fag: Masculinity and Sexuality in High School* (2007, University of California Press).

Justin Pickett is in the School of Criminal Justice at the University at Albany, SUNY. His research interests include public opinion on crime and criminal justice, social threat and social control, and juvenile justice and delinquency.

Francesca Polletta is in the sociology department at the University of California, Irvine. Her research interests include culture, politics, social movements, and law. She is the author of *It Was Like a Fever: Storytelling in Protest and Politics* (2006, University of Chicago Press) and *Freedom Is an Endless Meeting: Democracy in American Social Movements* (2002, University of Chicago Press).

Vincent Roscigno is in the sociology department at the Ohio State University. He is the author of *The Face of Discrimination:*

How Race and Gender Impact Work and Home Lives (2007, Rowman & Littlefield Publishers).

Amy Schalet is in the sociology department at the University of Massachusetts, Amherst. She is a specialist on adolescent sexuality and culture in comparative perspective. In addition to writing opinion pieces for *The New York Times* and *The Washington Post*, Schalet is the author of *Not Under My Roof: Parents, Teens, and the Culture of Sex* (2011, University of Chicago Press).

Naomi Sugie is in the criminology, law, and society department at the University of California, Irvine. She studies the consequences of incarceration and other forms of criminal justice contact for individuals and their romantic partners.

Daniel Sui is in the department of geography at the Ohio State University. His research interests include GIScience, social media, volunteered geographic information, health, and security implications of climate change.

Madison Van Oort is a PhD candidate in the sociology department at the University of Minnesota. She studies fast-fashion and low-wage labor in the twenty-first century.

Christopher Wildeman is in the department of policy analysis and management at Cornell University and is also co-director of the National Data Archive on Child Abuse and Neglect. His research focuses on the impact of mass incarceration, particularly on families and health. He is the co-author of *Children of the Prison Boom: Mass Incarceration and the Future of American Inequality* (2013, Oxford University Press).

index